Small-Produ
WOODWORKING
FOR THE
Home Shop

KERRY PIERCE

POPULAR WOODWORKING BOOKS

CINCINNATI, OHIO

Read This Important Safety Notice

To prevent accidents, keep safety in mind while you work. Use the safety guards installed on power equipment, keep fingers away from saw blades, wear safety goggles to prevent injuries from flying wood chips and sawdust, wear headphones to protect your hearing, and consider installing a dust vacuum to reduce the amount of airborne sawdust in your woodshop. Don't wear loose clothing, such as neckties or shirts with loose sleeves, or jewelry, such as rings, necklaces or bracelets, when working on power equipment. The author and editors who compiled this book have tried to make all the contents as accurate and correct as possible. Plans, illustrations, photographs and text have been carefully checked. All instructions, plans and projects should be carefully read, studied and understood before beginning construction. Due to the variability of local conditions, construction materials, skill levels, etc., neither the author nor Popular Woodworking Books assumes any responsibility for any accidents, injuries, damages or other losses incurred resulting from the material presented in this book.

METRIC CONVERSION CHART

TO CONVERT	TO	MULTIPLY BY
Inches	Centimeters	2.54
Centimeters	Inches	0.4
Feet	Centimeters	30.5
Centimeters	Feet	0.03

02 01 00 99 98   5 4 3 2 1

Library of Congress Cataloging-in-Publication Data

Pierce, Kerry.
   Small production woodworking for the home shop / by Kerry Pierce.
     p.   cm.
  Includes index.
  ISBN 1-55870-462-0 (alk. paper)
  1. Woodwork. 2. Production management. 3. Economic lot size. I. Title.
TT180.P5 1998
684'.08—dc21
                                                      97-49056
                                                        CIP

Content edited by Bruce Stoker
Production edited by Patrick G. Souhan
Interior designed by Brian Roeth
Photography pp. 36, 46 by Terry A. Jonasson
Photography p. 86 by Thomas R. Hartley

A variation of the chapter about the work of Judy Ditmer (pp. 100–112) appeared in *Woodwork* magazine.

Acknowledgments

Thanks:

Elaine, Emily, Andy.

Jim and Sally.

The many students whose presence in my classroom has permitted me to be a teacher: Jennifer, Chris, Kim, Lindsey, Vinnie, Jeff, Julie, Jennifer, Brenda, Tiff, Trish, Joan, Johnny, Jess, Jessie, Danny, D.J., Eric, Kitty, Kaite, Mo, Stacey, Caroline.

And Karen Wornock, ace librarian.

About the Author

Kerry Pierce has been a woodworker for more than twenty years, and holds a Master of Arts degree from Ohio University. Before becoming contributing editor of *Woodwork Magazine*, he spent fifteen years in a custom woodshop specialized in chair-making. Other magazines he has contributed to include *Woodshop News* and *Weekend Woodcraft*. He is the author of several books on woodworking, including *Making Elegant Gifts From Wood* (Betterway Books, 1996) and *The Art of Chair-Making* (Sterling, 1997). He resides in Lancaster, Ohio.

Table of Contents

CHAPTER ONE: **JOHN POLLOCK**

"There's a fine line between flaw and character."

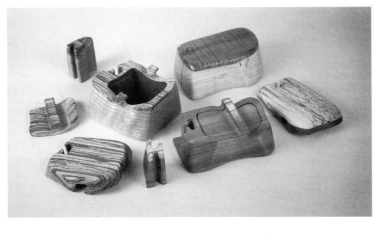

Single design or a series of one-of-a-kind pieces, understanding the process of design, construction and finishing will help you streamline your small production runs.

CHAPTER TWO: **PATRICK LEONARD**

"We all want to build that one awesome piece . . . but we also have to make a living."

By factoring precision design and construction into the process, you will no longer have to sacrifice beauty for machine-quick production runs.

Once you develop a system for producing your projects, constant re-evaluation and occasional reinvestment in tooling and your shop will help you fine-tune the process toward maximum efficiency.

"I was always reinvesting."

Capitalize on all your interests, experiences and strengths, and add them to your production processes for additional efficiency and enjoyment.

"As a patternmaker, I could make almost anything out of wood. That was great training."

When your work is fun or a "labor of love," it's easier to find the flaws in the product or the system and then correct them for a better product or production run.

"It's fun to see kids play with the toys."

"We could do it this way . . . or that way—what's going to be easier?"

Designing jigs and fixtures to expedite and simplify procedures is at the heart of production run efficiency.

"There's always something else that needs doing."

A workstation aids the production run by dividing procedures into more manageable tasks, breaking up the monotony of repetivie work and utilizing shop space more efficiently.

"Woodworking is much easier and accurate than it used to be, thanks to technology."

While there is an inherent, universal appeal to handcrafted work, it is often too time intensive to be efficient in production runs. Determine where you can benefit from technology without sacrificing that appeal.

Sometimes flexibility needs to be built into a production run to allow for innovation, experimentation and the occasional "glitch."

"To carve an elephant, you take a block of wood and cut away everything that's not part of the elephant."

Consider the suggestions in this summary chapter to help add production runs in your own shop.

Preface

Why production runs?

Why not focus your creative energies on one-of-a-kind construction?

The answer is simple: Woodworkers—like the men and women who toil at other, more mainstream trades—have to eat, and unless your reputation puts you at the very top of the woodworking food chain, unless your last name is Maloof or Castle or Krenov, unless you're represented by tony uptown galleries, you must find ways to produce your work at prices modest enough to appeal to the men and women who, like yourself, have to work for a living.

Production runs help make that possible.

Quality control is another benefit of production runs. Think about it: If your car needs a new transmission, do you take it to the well-meaning neighbor who, although he's done a lot of work on his own car, has never lifted the hood of a 1994 Caprice like the one you drive? Or do you take your car to the specialist who's put a hundred transmissions into cars just like yours? The answer is simple: You choose the specialist because his experience improves your chances of getting the job done right.

Production runs make it possible for you to become a specialist in the woodshop. They make it possible for you to acquire the experience that can lead to a consistently high level of quality. If you make 50 six-drawer jewelry boxes, you quickly become expert in the creation of those jewelry boxes. You quickly acquire more experience with the manufacture of that particular design than the craftsman who, however skilled he may be, makes just one of those boxes. This experience can lead to a level of quality that the best one-of-a-kind craftsperson will struggle to duplicate.

Production runs are also important shop aids for those woodworkers who have no interest in turning their hobby into a profession.

Suppose you've designed a handsome candle box with dovetailed corners and a sliding lid. Suppose you've decided that this candle box will make a great Christmas gift for all your cousins and nieces. Do you really want to make them one at a time, repeating all the necessary machine setups for each candle box?

Maybe not. Maybe you'll want to make those candle boxes quickly and efficiently, reusing machine setups and carving pulls with a pantograph-directed router. That way you'll have time to enjoy a leisurely Thanksgiving meal with your family.

Introduction

I began this book with a set of expectations. I expected, for example, to describe lots of jigs and fixtures. However, although there are some present (turn to chapter six on the work of Jody Gray Chapman for some elegant examples), I found that many woodworkers who use production runs in their daily operations make little use of these shop aids. In some cases, the nature of the product they manufacture doesn't lend itself to jigs and fixtures. In other cases, the personality of the craftsperson (John Pollock, chapter one, is one example) requires a less rigid approach than jigs and fixtures allow.

I expected, too, that I would discuss the clever strategies with which these crafts-people move material into, through and out of their shops. But although the crafts-people I interviewed are without exception talented and creative, displaying great ingenuity in their work and in the methods by which they create that work, none see the storage and movement of material as critical to their operations. Patrick Leonard (chapter two) stores his lumber in a small building next to his basement shop and carries it into his shop when it's needed. Ray Muniak (chapter four) stores his in a set of enormous drawers under his workbenches. Judy Ditmer (chapter nine) stores much of her turning stock outside, in the weather, under a layer of wet shavings. Jody Gray Chapman moves her material from one operation to the next on wheeled carts. And Bill Saling (chapter seven) carries his from workstation to workstation in his hands, up and down rough, wooden steps, on a hillside, often in the dark. Although effective, there's nothing innovative about these methods of handling material.

The one exception to this might be some recent developments in the shop of Warren May (chapter eight). Warren has taken a hard look at the issue of scrap and now makes use of the many rips and cutoffs left behind after the manufacture of dulcimers and Kentucky furniture produced in his shop, turning material he once gave away as firewood into cutting boards, treenware and small finger-jointed boxes. This solution to the scrap problem works for Warren because he already has a gallery through which he sells his work, and these small items have been added to the line he carries in that gallery. A craftsperson who doesn't own a gallery might find this idea more troublesome to implement.

I also expected this book to describe lots of really beefy, industrial-grade machinery, and there is some present on these pages. For example, Jim Anderson's operation (chapter three) is dependent upon some of the largest and most powerful woodworking equipment I've ever seen. Ed Schmidt, too, has created a shop designed around the capabilities of some large and sophisticated equipment (chapter five). His pneumatic clamping table is one notable example. In fact, to keep himself up-to-date on the issues of equipment and technology, Ed makes annual visits to the big woodworking expo held every other year in Atlanta.

But more common are shops like those of Ray Muniak or Bill Saling. In these shops, production-run work is accomplished on the same kind of equipment that can be found in any Sears store in the country.

I also expected some revelations on the subject of parts flow through the shop. But here again I was surprised. Yes, Patrick Leonard does track the progress of his work through the use of computer printouts, but for the most part, the craftspeople I interviewed just *know* what needs to be done next. This knowledge isn't achieved through meticulous planning. In most cases, it's just part of the continuing evolution of shop practices that I saw in every shop I visited.

Bill Saling's methods probably best represent this intuitive approach to parts flow. His work moves back and forth, up- and downhill, from one building to the next, from one room to the next, in a dizzying pattern I couldn't hope to explain with absolute clarity. But Bill knows. He doesn't have to write it down. He just knows, and more important, his method works. It permits him to deliver the appropriate parts to the appropriate locations at the appropriate times.

So what did I learn during six months of visiting the shops of some of the most successful craftspeople in the Ohio Valley? First, I learned it's impossible to generalize about the methods by which different craftspeople utilize production runs in their operations. Each individual craftsperson brings to his or her work a set of abilities and life experiences which, in large part, determine that craftsperson's approach to the use of production runs.

I learned, for example, that John Pollock's approach is focused on manual skill, speed at the band saw, and the free-form nature of his boxes. His approach best suits his personality.

I learned that Patrick Leonard enjoys precision work, and as a result, his use of the production run is focused on meticulous planning and careful machine setups.

I learned that Jim Anderson loves big machinery, and designs products and processes that require this machinery.

I learned that, like Jim Anderson, Ed Schmidt has an abiding love for big machines, which expresses itself not only in the manner in which he works, but also in the objects he creates: wooden bulldozers, steam shovels, concrete trucks.

I learned that Jody Gray Chapman, like her uncle before her, enjoys the creation of simple, clean lines—a pleasure evident in both the objects she creates and in the methods by which she creates them.

I learned that Warren May's approach to the dulcimer is based on an intimate knowledge of the materials he works with and of the musical instruments he builds— a knowledge he has acquired through 25 years of experimentation.

I learned that Bill Saling's artistic background requires an approach to craftwork

that permits him to express his artistic bent in the gentle caricature which character-
izes his dancers.

I learned that Judy Ditmer allows the design of each piece of wooden jewelry to
evolve as she turns and shapes the bits of wood that will eventually become earrings,
pendants and pins.

Finally, I learned this from Ray Muniak, another maker of wooden jewelry:

"People are always asking me how they can make what I make," Ray told me as
we talked in his shop one cold, November day. "You know what I tell them? I tell
them that if their grandfather didn't have red hair, they can't make what I make."

Ray laughed, but I must have looked puzzled because he went on to explain,
"Everything I do is a result of every experience I've had. If I hadn't been a patternmaker for 15 years, I would work differently. If I hadn't seen that first piece of lath
art in San Francisco, I wouldn't be doing what I am today. If I didn't work in this
particular shop, I would work differently.

"What I tell people when they ask me that question is that they shouldn't try to
make what I make; they should make what *they* make."

And that, I think, is the theme of this book.

We would be unlikely to succeed if we attempted to manufacture John Pollock's
band-sawn boxes or Warren May's dulcimers or Patrick Leonard's small chests. Those
products are direct results of the personalities and life experiences of the craftsmen
who created them. However, we can learn much from their manufacturing methods
that we can apply in our own work.

In that vein, I offer this book *not* as a prescription for what must be done to
utilize production runs in your own shop. Instead, I offer this book as an assortment
of suggestions. Here you will see what I saw when I visited the shops of these craftspeople. Here you will see how these individuals carry out their production work. And
while it's unlikely either you or I will use the exact procedures I saw in any individual
shop, we will see, if we look carefully, ideas in every chapter that we can adapt to
the work we wish to accomplish in our own shops.

CHAPTER ONE

JOHN POLLOCK

Understanding the Process

John's boxes are designed around several themes. First, because of his freehand approach at the band saw, no two boxes are alike. Second, he makes extensive use of contrasting wood: Notice the mixture of light and dark woods, of native and tropical woods, of plain and figured woods. And third, with most of the models he sells, John includes a separate, inner lid—a feature not often found in boxes made by his competitors.

Notice, too, the flocking on the interior walls of each box.

FOCUS: Although he often works in production runs numbering more than 70 pieces, no two of John Pollock's band-sawn boxes are alike. His success is based on two principles: (1) Manual skill, particularly on the band saw, makes production work possible; and (2) The free-form nature of his boxes permits the rapid creation of one-of-a-kind items.

I t's hard to take John Pollock's picture. He's in constant motion, hands blurred, parts flying. By the time I move the tripod into one position and focus my camera, John's disappeared from the viewfinder, darting off into some other area of the shop, already involved in the next step in his production process.

But I persevere, following him from one location to another, each time setting up my camera more quickly, ultimately abandoning the tripod altogether, relying instead on handheld shots. Then, when even this doesn't work, I ask him to hold still. And although he does oblige, I sense he feels something unnatural in his stillness, as if just below the surface, undetectable by the camera or the human eye, there is a quivering, humming anticipation of the shutter's release and thereby his own release from the constraints of even momentary stillness.

"How many stores are there where you can wholesale toys?"

"My first woodworking experience came when my daughter—who is now 21—had her first birthday. I made a rocking horse for her. We were living then in an apartment, so it was all handwork. I did it with coping saws and hand drills—just very basic hand tools.

"I still have that horse around here." John laughs, something he does often and well. "I once had an opportunity to sell it, but my daughter had a conniption.

"I made toys for my kids, and various friends said, 'Well, how about making some for my kids?'

"So I started doing some local (Toledo area) shows, selling just wooden toys.

"I made toys for quite a while. Then I decided to try a show that wasn't in the Toledo area. Here, at the local shows, I might make a few dollars. Then I went down to Cincinnati's Summerfair, and I did extremely well there.

"When I got home, I said, 'Gosh, this

is fun, and I made some money.' I thought if I could get into enough of these good shows, and forget the crummy shows, I could maybe make a living at this."

At that time, John was a car salesman by day, a toymaker by night. "At the dealership, I worked Monday nights and Thursday nights until 9:00 P.M., and the rest of the week, I worked till 5:00 P.M. And every night after work, even on Monday and Thursday nights, I would come home, change clothes, go downstairs and make toys. Then about 11:00 P.M. I'd come upstairs, eat a little something while I watched the news. Then I'd go to bed and get up and start all over again the next day."

John begins a run of boxes by cutting the material to the approximate length of the finished boxes. The resulting shorts are then stacked on shelves until he is ready to begin a gluing session.

"How many stores are there where you can wholesale toys?"

Some of John's most popular boxes employ burl. Shown here are some of the burl slabs he will eventually cut into box bodies or lids.

"I've got one daughter in college at the University of Cincinnati. I've got another daughter who will be in college next year. And what I do here," John indicates his shop with a wave of his hand, "will help pay for their educations."

He shakes his head. "I can't see me selling cars again. I figure I'll go on here until I die. I enjoy it too much."

After several years of making and selling toys, John decided to switch to puzzle boxes for what he saw as several very good reasons. First, doing a show with the types of toys John was then selling involved a great deal of manual labor. "I used to carry between 27 and 35 banana boxes of toys to each show, and for all practical purposes, those toys were solid wood, which made the boxes very heavy."

Second, John wanted to insulate his business from the whims of the individuals who juried the arts-and-crafts shows. "There's a lot of politics that go into the process of getting into arts-and-crafts shows. If you're doing the better shows—which are strictly juried by slides—you never know whether you're going to get in or not. And while I've always been fortunate enough to get into some very, very good shows, I began to wonder what would happen if one year I didn't. You know, all of a sudden you don't have that money you got from those shows.

"So I decided to go wholesale, and although there aren't many places where you can wholesale toys, I figured that in any big town there might be four or five stores that might carry my boxes—gift shops, galleries, jewelry stores. So I took a look at puzzle boxes."

But the most important factor in John's decision to switch from toys to puzzle boxes was the ages of his children. "My kids were growing up. They were getting into summer softball and things like that, and when I relied on the

As John considered the possibility of doing shows full-time, he spoke to some people who were then doing it professionally. "Some wouldn't give me the time of day, but others would tell me which shows were good and which I should steer away from."

Then one day he quit his job at the dealership, leaving behind the safety of conventional employment, and became a full-time toy maker. "It's true that I don't have the same kind of security I would have with a regular job, but at the same time, if I find myself in a situation where I need to pick up some extra money, I just find another customer or I work a little harder or I do another craft show.

retail shows, I was always on the road." In this regard John's decision has paid the richest dividends. "I ended up coaching softball for nine or ten years, and that's something I wouldn't have been able to do if I'd continued with the retail shows."

"The trick is to find the right niche, to find the right product that you can make and sell at the right price."

John leans back in his ancient desk chair, hands shuffling a pair of ¼"-thick hardwood blocks as if they were playing cards. "A friend of mine called me up and said, 'I got a young guy who wants to get into woodworking and doing shows. He's very good at doing exact work, precise work.'

"So I sat down with him [the young guy] and his wife. I told them the pros and the cons and all that good stuff. Then we looked at his ideas for products. He has some really good ideas, but some of them are too complicated. He can't make them for the price he would have to put on them to expect any sales.

"But there are a lot of niches out there. The trick is to find the right one.

"People starting off have more trouble with pricing than with any other part of the business. They underprice. They don't think that they are, but they're not considering everything. When you start out and you're coming up with a wholesale price and a retail price, you have to take everything into consideration—wood, shop rent, telephone, labor. Even if you're getting your material free, you have to figure the cost as if you're buying it. Otherwise, when you do have to buy it, your customers will be looking at a large price increase that could kill your sales."

Although by the time John had begun making boxes he knew he wanted to wholesale, his actual entry into that segment of the business came about almost by accident. "I had loaded a friend's store

with boxes, just wall to wall, and one time when I was going up to check on them, I ran into a sales rep. Nobody introduced us, and I don't know how I knew he was a sales rep. I mean, he just looked like one. So I went over and introduced myself, and it turned out that that's what he was, a sales rep." John laughs with undisguised delight at the memory.

"He was out of Grand Rapids, Michigan. We got to talking, and I told him I was thinking about getting a sales rep.

"He sold my line for a while—mostly to galleries and jewelry stores. In fact, he opened up some good accounts which I still have."

As John became more established, he weaned his business from its reliance on sales reps. In part, this was a reaction to the insistence of one of his sales reps that he change his product line to please a new group of potential customers. But an even more important reason for the change was John's realization that he no longer needed that kind of representation. As more of his boxes spread across the country, more and more new accounts approached him directly, having seen his work at another shop or in someone's home. "Somebody who owns a store somewhere else in the country

This is John's first assembly table. The shorts (shown stacked on the shelves in photo 1) are glued and stacked to the height of the finished boxes. Each stack is then clamped into one of the vises ringing this table. Additional clamping is provided by the pipe clamps and C-clamps laid beside each vise.

"The trick is to find the right niche, to find the right product that you can make and sell at the right price."

John has fixed a stack of shorts in a bench vise. He is completing the clamping process with a pair of pipe clamps.

will happen into a store in, maybe San Francisco that carries my boxes. They'll see my stuff and inquire, and the owner of that store in San Francisco will give the guy my name.

"If I hear from that new store and I think I've got a real good chance to get that account, I'll send them a piece. And I'll say, 'This is yours. You don't have to send it back. This is the kind of stuff I make.'"

Today, John is cautious about opening

up new accounts. "I stay away from the big chains like Pier 1 Imports or the Nature Company. I just can't keep up with that kind of demand."

He's also careful to respect the needs of existing customers when he opens new accounts. "First, I look at where they're at. If I've already got an account in that town, I'll call up my account and say, 'Listen. I've got an inquiry from XYZ.'

"In some cases, this new business might be a direct competitor of my existing account. They might even be just around the corner. But in other cases, I'll call my existing account and they'll say the new business is clear on the other side of town, they're good people, they've got a nice store, it's not going to hurt us if you sell to them, too."

He's also cautious about doing retail shows in cities where he has accounts. "In fact, I try to avoid doing a show in a town where I have an established customer. I may call them and ask permission. For example, I've got a real good account in Midland, Michigan. Now, I used to do a show in Midland and did real well there, but once this store started ordering from

The front and both ends of the box are cut with the band saw table set at 11°. After he's cut the front and both ends on a number of boxes, he will reset the band saw table to 0° and saw the backs.

This operation has two functions: First, it evens up the edges of the glued-up shorts. Second, the undulating band-sawn surface adds sculptural interest to the piece.

John draws no lines on the material prior to sawing. All four sides of the box are defined freehand, a practice John's enormous experience at creating free-form shapes on the band saw makes possible.

me—and they've ordered a lot of merchandise—I stopped doing the show. My focus is really on wholesale sales."

He's understandably meticulous about maintaining good relationships with his wholesale customers. "I do things a little differently than some guys. First, I don't have minimum [quantity] orders. Second, I don't have minimum [quantity] reorders.

"I've got an account that one year bought over 1000 boxes, and he started off with just 2 pieces. And he has since told me that if I hadn't sold him those first two pieces, he would have never bought from me. And maybe a store just got a new order in, and they've got 20, 25, 30 pieces sitting there, and a customer comes in and looks at a box and says, 'I like this box and I like this size, but this is the wood that I want it in.' If you've got a two- or three-hundred dollar minimum, that store's not going to reorder that special box.

"And I always exchange stuff—even if it's got a nick in it. Odds are I can fix it. And these services make a difference. I think they make my customers feel pretty good."

Doing Retail Shows

"I think originally I checked a publication called Crafts Report. *It's a newspaper-type publication. It's like* Sunshine Artists. *It has a listing of different shows."*

Although his focus is clearly on the wholesale segment of his business, John still does a handful of retail shows each year for several very good reasons. First, these shows are an excellent source of extra cash. "A couple of years ago, when my oldest daughter went away to college, I decided to do a couple of extra shows to help pay for that. But I've limited myself to one in May, one in June and one in July."

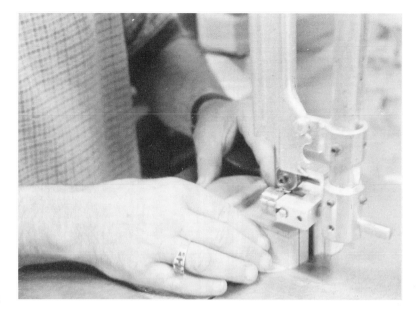

Here John is sawing (again freehand) the block that he just cut from the heart of the box. In this way, he will create another box that will rest within the main cavity of the completed box.

Second, the retail shows provide John with a way of making contact with potential wholesale customers.

Third, the shows are an important source of feedback from the buying public. Because he has no direct contact with the individuals who buy his boxes at the many shops and galleries that carry his work, he doesn't get to hear firsthand what those customers think about his choice of woods, shapes and textures. Retail shows provide him with invaluable firsthand contact with the public.

And retail shows can pay off in a big way. "I did the Ann Arbor Street Fair once and did extremely well. It was the best show I ever did."

Sometimes an individual customer can make the difference between an adequate show and an outstanding show. "At one show up in Michigan a couple came up to my booth and started picking up boxes. She'd load his arms, and he'd come over to my table, dump the stuff off and go back for more. And they never turned a box over to look at the price. So I'm thinking they're going to faint when they hear the price on all this stuff. Then, when they were done, I gave them the price, and he just reached into his pocket and handed over the cash."

"I think originally I checked a publication called *Crafts Report*. It's a newspaper-type publication. It's like *Sunshine Artists*. It has a listing of different shows."

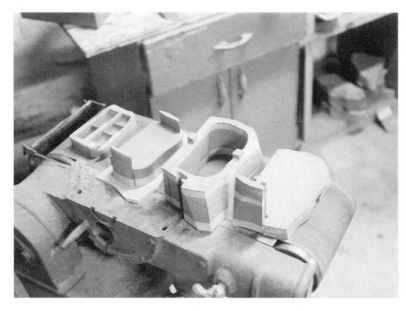

Shown are the various components of a freshly sawn box.

"I think you have to find something you love to do. It's not like I dread coming to work in the morning. If anything, my problem is leaving the shop."

A factor in John's decreasing reliance on the retail show is what he sees as the changing nature of the show circuit. "I don't think any of the old-timers will tell you that the retail show business is better than it used to be. There are more shows, but some have gotten greedy. For instance, where there once might have been 150 exhibitors, now there might be 300. And the pie gets chopped up into smaller and smaller pieces.

"There are still good shows out there, but at some of these shows you might have 2000 applicants for 150 spaces, which greatly reduces your odds of getting in. This is especially true if the show has a good reputation."

Experienced exhibitors, like John, may have a better chance of getting into a good show simply because they understand the process. "The real key to getting into a good show is having good slides because you're only going to be viewed for 10 or 15 seconds. So you have to make a good impression, and you have to do it quickly."

Although the money can be good, the show process is very demanding. "In the morning, I get up, go to the show and set up. This takes me 45 minutes to an hour if I have help. And you know people are going to come early, so for a nine o'clock show you've got to start getting ready before seven o'clock. And although the show may technically end at 9:00 P.M., nobody leaves by then. So by the time you actually get stuff put away, it's 11:00 P.M. or later, and you still haven't had dinner. After three or four days of this, I'm just shot."

A run of 25 freshly sawn boxes are stacked in the left foreground. The various subassemblies are then glued together at this table. (Notice the school of spring clamps feeding on the edge of the table.)

"I think you have to find something you love to do. It's not like I dread coming to work in the morning. If anything, my problem is leaving the shop."

The number of hours John spends in his shop is, in part, determined by the number of interruptions he experiences. "My friends sometimes forget this is my livelihood. Yesterday I had people here for three or four hours, and I was out here cutting. If I've got stuff that's got to be done, I just have to do it, even if I've got people here in the shop."

The seasons can also help to determine the length of John's workweek. "During the months before Christmas, I'm out here seven days a week, morning, noon and night. Then I crash for about a week after Christmas."

Through the rest of the year, John does try to keep regular hours, coming in early in the morning and leaving late in the afternoon. Safety is one important reason for limiting the number of hours he works. "Once, when I was still selling cars, I had a real close call. I had worked until 9:00 P.M. at the car lot. Then I came home, changed clothes, and went down into the basement to work until 11:00 P.M. I was making toys at the time, and on this night, I was putting spare tires on little wooden cars. I had a 2′ length of dowel I was using as an axle, but instead of cutting it off on the band saw, I took out a chip knife and I put the dowel against the bench. Then, while cutting the dowel, I slipped and nearly cut my right ring finger off. I did cut into the bone, severing the flexor tendons. I had to have surgery, and I spent two days in the hospital.

"And I had a close call on the band saw a couple of weeks ago. I was cutting the outsides on some boxes. I usually cut the outsides at 11°, 12° or 13°, but I was cutting them at 45°. I was tired, and I was doing something unfamiliar, and I slipped and plowed into my finger—my own fault."

The various subassemblies are spring lamped together and stacked so all subassemblies from one box are in the same stack.

John has experimented with hired help. In fact there is a time clock hanging from the wall beside his cluttered desk. "I tried it, but when I took a big order and crunch time came, my help would call in sick. Or they'd go out and get plastered.

"And quality was an issue too. I found I had to go over every piece and make sure it was okay before I finished it.

"So I said, 'The heck with it.' I decided to get my prices up there where I could make a little bit of a living and just go with the flow."

Making the Product

"There's a fine line between flaw and character."

Not many professionals make puzzle boxes, and John believes each craftsperson's work, including his own, can be distinguished from all other makers' puzzle boxes by paying attention to a few key details.

"You've got Richard Rothbart; he's the old-timer. There's a guy in New England who does really complicated things. There's one in Cincinnati. There's

"There's a fine line between flaw and character."

John uses several power sanders to remove band saw marks. The belt sander is used for flat sanding.

another guy in Washington or Oregon and a few in California. There's me.

"But we all do something different. Yes, the boxes are all made on the band saw, but if you really look at them, you see that each guy has a style. The guy in Cincinnati does a couple of pieces that are real puzzles. It's tough to get into the boxes. Mine are a bit more simplified in that regard. I don't make mine where they're real hard to get apart or to get back together."

John identifies several details that make his boxes different from others. One is his use of exotic and mixed woods. "Puzzle boxes have been around for thousands of years, probably originating in China or Japan—somewhere in that part of the world—but most of the ones I'd seen at the time I started were solid wood. So I decided to mix things up. Where a lot of guys make a whole box out of zebrawood, I decided a piece of zebrawood looks better sitting on a piece of black walnut or a piece of cherry or even a piece of oak."

John also uses a lot of burl in his work, particularly buckeye burl, which he buys from a source he refuses to divulge. Sometimes he allows the top of the box to reveal the wildly irregular, natural surface of the burl. "I had a woman once who picked up

a box—a beautiful box with a lot of character in the wood—and she said, 'Is this one cheaper because it's flawed?' I laughed and said, 'It isn't flawed, it has character, and there is a difference.' "

His boxes also differ from the competition's in their inclusion of a second interior lid covering the main compartment. It takes a bit more time to produce, but John believes details like this have enabled his boxes to remain salable.

He sculpts the exterior of each box a bit more than most of his competitors do. In order to include this characteristic and remain competitively priced, John developed methods to create these shapes with a few quick cuts on the band saw, finishing the surfaces with a power sander. "I tilt the table on my band saw to about 11°." He then does some free-form cutting on the front and both ends of the boxes, usually leaving the back, which will be hinged, perpendicular to the band saw table. He then sands the undulating sides and front with his drum sanders.

Occasionally, he even makes boxes to order. "I had a woman who had a ferret. Actually, she had two ferrets, but the one had just died, and she wanted a box to put the ferret's ashes in. And she wanted a box with two cavities. The ashes from the ferret that had just died would go in one cavity. Then later, when the other ferret died, its ashes would go in the other cavity."

Streamlining Production

"I've tried to keep track of the true time a box takes."

In any woodshop production run, material is the first consideration. John doesn't buy much locally. "Toledo used to have a good place to buy cherry, maple, walnut—all the domestic woods—but they went out of business. The

> "I've tried to keep track of the true time a box takes."

places that are around now are just too expensive. Through trial and error, I ended up with L. L. Johnson out of Charlotte, Michigan. They carry both domestics and a lot of exotics. When I go up there, I'll spend about a thousand dollars."

After crosscutting his material to the approximate overall lengths of the various boxes, John mixes and matches blocks of wood. "I'll take a piece of zebrawood and glue it on top of something else. Or I'll glue a piece of burl onto a piece of cherry. I'll do a whole stack of these at one time, maybe 10 or 20. Then I'll go on to something else."

When he's accumulated a supply of glued-up blocks, usually around a hundred, he moves to the band saw. Here, using a ¼″ blade he defines the back of the box in one quick pass with the table set 90° from the blade. After he's cut a large number of backs, he resets the table so that it's 10° or 11° from the perpendicular and begins to cut fronts and sides.

He then resets the band saw to 90° and slices the bottom off.

Next, he replaces the band saw's ¼″

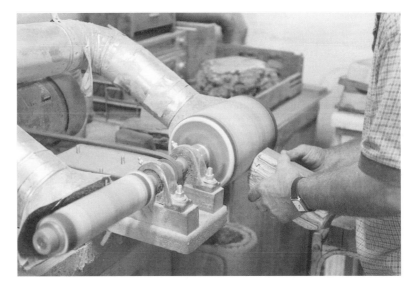

The pneumatic drum sander makes quick work of sanding contoured or round sections.

blade with a ⅛″ blade and cuts the puzzle piece or the lock.

He then turns the box on its side, cuts the lid off, then cuts out the inside cavity along with any trays or compartments.

When this operation is complete, he moves to his gluing room. "Some use weights to clamp the subassemblies together. I use Pony spring clamps."

Because he cuts all of his boxes freehand, the parts are not interchangeable. The interior compartments from one box will not fit into any other. Therefore, John

John's hands blur as he removes spring clamps from glued subassemblies.

John guides glued-up blocks past the blade of his band saw, creating the outside contours of his boxes.

is careful to keep together all the interior components of one box as it moves through the shop. He speaks ruefully about occasions when he's dropped a stack of unglued boxes while transferring them from his machinery room to his gluing room, thereby mixing their many parts.

After gluing and clamping the interior compartments, he is careful to stack together all the glued and clamped components of a particular box.

When the glue has cured, the box, with its various interior subassemblies, is taken back into the machining room for sanding.

John first rough sands the entire box with an 80-grit belt on a stationary drum sander. He then moves to his pneumatic drum sanders, smoothing surfaces with 150-grit paper, then with 320-grit paper.

The box is then disassembled and the parts are flap sanded with 180-grit slashed paper to ease all sharp edges. He finishes sanding with 600-grit paper, which polishes most woods. The box is then ready for its hand-rubbed oil finish.

Because, even with a dust collection system, sanding can be an unpleasant experience, John tries to avoid long periods of unrelieved sanding. "I'll do 10 or 20 at a time at one station. Then I'll do other things—cutting, gluing, whatever."

Unlike some other makers of puzzle boxes, John doesn't sand the band sawn interior surfaces of his boxes. Instead, he flocks them, which is much quicker and produces a more finished appearance. Flocking—the application of bits of dyed fiber to give surfaces a velvetlike appearance—can be done very quickly. After an adhesive has been applied to the interior surfaces of a box, John applies the flocking. "I got one of those crop-duster-type sprayers. It makes a difference in the quality of the finished product."

When the flocking is dry, John rubs out the exterior of the box with #0000 steel wool and applies a coat of paste wax.

Understanding the Process

At the heart of John's success in the use of the production run is his fluid speed at the band saw. The experience he's gained through the creation of thousands of puzzle boxes has given him an almost uncanny comprehension of the forms he creates. In mere seconds, without any preliminary drawing or conscious planning, he can render a thick block of solid wood into the various interior components of a nested puzzle box. And the box will work. After sanding, gluing and more sanding, the box will come together in a form that intrigues with its engineering, delights with its figured and contrasting woods, and pleases with its simple but satisfying aesthetics.

CHAPTER TWO

The Beauty of the Machine

The design of this chest was influenced by the Japanese.

FOCUS: Patrick Leonard produces small case pieces in production runs of between 6 and 20 copies. These production runs are designed around two principles: (1) Immaculate design and engineering are essential to the production run process; and (2) High-tech equipment allows the craftsperson to create high-quality work in a timely fashion.

When the phone rings in Patrick Leonard's shop near Washington, Pennsylvania, he steps into his backyard away from the noise of his machinery and his dust collection system and pulls a cellular phone from his back pocket. When he travels to the wholesale shows that generate the bulk of his business, he takes with him a Gateway laptop with CD-ROM, stereo sound and 1.2 gigabytes of memory. He tracks the movement of orders through his shop with the aid of a constantly updated computer printout. His imaginatively designed chests and boxes are engineered around the high-tech capabilities of his commercial-grade woodworking machinery.

Patrick believes in the efficiencies of the small shop production run, specifically in those efficiencies made possible by the technologies now available to the professional woodworker.

"This is the perfect setting for a woodshop."

His driveway is a challenge, and my van strains to negotiate its steep inclines. The surface is gravel, pitted with saucepan-sized washouts. It climbs rapidly from Alamae Lakes Road through a stand of young trees, past the green lawn surrounding the two-story house Patrick built with his own hands. Above each front window and the thick, oak, frame and panel entrance door—also made by Patrick—is a scroll-sawn cartouche, painted the same pale burgundy as the natural color of the Maryland sandstone used to lay up the chimney. The cartouches and the gallery of turned spindles surrounding the front porch verify that this is, indeed, the home of a woodworker.

I ease the van to a stop on the gravel apron beside the house. Stepping down, I take in the scenery. The land falls away in all directions. Trees define the horizon.

A three-year-old boy with extraordinarily curly brown hair careens around the corner of the house toward me, arms pinwheeling, a grin smeared across his face. Following behind, I see Patrick, tall and thin with a half-inch length of beard encircling his face. Patrick and I shake hands, and he introduces his son, Kyle. The boy positions himself directly in my path and begins to speak at light speed, his face lit by a radiant grin. I think he's asking me something about my van.

Another boy, a year or two older than Kyle, appears. Although his hair is red, it too is very curly. Ian also beams in my direction.

Accompanied by the two boys, Patrick first escorts me to the woodshed, a small frame building set close to the back side of the house. Opening a wooden latch, clearly made by hand, he throws back the doors and inside I see neat stacks of hardwood lumber, some rising almost to the ceiling. I see bird's-eye maple and purpleheart. I see cherry in several thicknesses and thick planks of plain maple. "I used to store firewood in here," Patrick explains, "but I needed the space for lumber. So now I stack the firewood in the yard." We sort through a few boards on the top of one stack.

Patrick stands near his wood storage building.

"This is the perfect setting for a woodshop."

Most of Patrick's material is stored in this small building, which is just a few steps from the door of his shop.

> "At this point, the business is doing so well I'm having trouble keeping up."

Examining the Shop

We move on to his shop, which is situated in the basement of his home. It's large, airy and equipped with high-tech and very expensive commercial-grade machinery. A huge abrasive planer stands just inside the door. A Mini Max table saw outfitted with a Biesemeyer fence and a beefy power feeder occupies the center of the room. The shop also houses a band saw, a lathe, a mortising machine and a planer. A sheet metal cyclone stands in one corner.

Everything looks brand new. Everything looks expensive.

More lumber is stored on a metal rack along the back wall of the shop. I recognize walnut and more purpleheart. I also see several tropical species I can't identify.

Discussing the Business

Later, sitting in the shade on the grass outside his home, we talk about Patrick's woodworking business.

Patrick shows me several with particularly dense swirls of bird's-eyes.

"At this point, the business is doing so well I'm having trouble keeping up."

"I've been woodworking all my life. I started off with a circular saw and a hammer. This was when I was 12." Patrick, unlike most children drawn to woodworking, had to learn on his own. "I never had a father, so nobody ever showed me how to do this stuff. It was all me. A lot of trial and error.

"I went to college. In fact I have a bachelor of science degree in psychology, but even during my time in college, I was doing woodworking to make extra money. My academic goal was to become a psychologist, but woodworking just drew me in. And I think I'm a much happier person than I would have been if I'd gone into psychology."

Patrick credits his wife, Eileen, with making it possible for him to become a professional woodworker. "She works, and she was able to keep us going financially during my transition into full-time professional woodworking.

"A lot of woodworkers don't make that transition because they can't say, 'OK, I just won't make any money for a year while I get myself established.' For most guys that's just impossible."

Eileen, who made that possible for Patrick by working for Blue Cross/Blue Shield, is more experienced in the field of business than Patrick is, and he would like someday to more fully use her talents in his woodworking operation. "Eventually, when my business gets established a little more solidly, I'd like her to leave her job and work with me."

Growing the Business

Although he began as a maker of custom cabinets, he disliked the difficulties of building to suit his customers. As a result, he changed his business so that he now sells—primarily to the various galleries who have approached him after seeing his work at wholesale shows—only those pieces that appear in his six-page, full-color catalog. This procedure not only protects him from the whims of the individuals who order custom work, it also permits Patrick to capitalize on the efficiencies of the production-run process.

"I think we all want to build that one awesome piece of furniture, but we also have to make a living."

"With me, there's never any middle stage. I dive into things headfirst. I have a game plan, and I think about the game plan, and I go for it. I started with the idea of selling to a broad range of customers. I wanted to sell to galleries across the country, and I wanted to do a few retail shows."

Like many other woodworking professionals, Patrick recognized the difficulties of handling large-scale furniture at the various shows he wanted to do. He was concerned that the expense of crating, shipping and renting booth space for beds or tables or armoires would eat too deeply into his profits. "I think it's difficult to do this with really nice, full-size furniture.

"I wanted to sell nice things, but you can't handle a bedroom set in a $10' \times 10'$ booth, so I downscaled. I went to smaller pieces—pieces that I could sell out of my booth on a cash-and-carry basis.

"I started out with a couple of retail shows, just to get my feet wet. I think there the sales weren't as important as observing the people's reactions to my pieces. It isn't the same crowd that you get at the galleries, but you get to hear comments. Someone will say, 'I like this wood,' or, 'I don't like this wood.' At one retail show a couple of years ago, a guy stopped at my booth and said, 'You know, cigars are starting to get real big. You might want to consider building humidors.' And now humidors are a huge part of my business."

His relationship with the various galleries that now account for nearly all his sales began with several wholesale shows. "Calling the galleries on the phone does not work. To be able to attain any kind of credibility, you need to do the shows. They see you there. They place the orders. It's a pretty simple process at the shows.

"I did the ACC [American Craft Council] show in Baltimore. I did a couple in Philadelphia, one in Columbus."

The biggest problem Patrick has encountered with the wholesale shows has been avoiding the temptation to sell to too many galleries. He ruefully describes a competitive drive to sell to them all. "Right now, I have orders from over a hundred galleries, and I don't know how I'm going to keep up. I don't even want to think about the number of pieces I have to produce in the next couple of months.

"In that sense, my business is a success. I have lots of work, but I'm having trouble meeting all the commitments I've made. When you add in the business side, which we woodworkers tend to despise, it's overwhelming. And that's where I hope my wife can come into the picture. She'll do the accounting, the billing, keeping track of all the orders I need to get out."

In addition to the problems of construction and accounting, Patrick also must deal with the issue of shipping his pieces all over the country. "There's a cardboard-box maker here locally, but I have to order in decent quantities. I have to buy 250 at a time, and at a buck to two bucks apiece, that's a pretty good investment. And each piece I ship is double boxed." This precaution, although protective of his work, is not only expensive in terms of material, it is also expensive in terms of time. Too, he must find space for the various-sized boxes his work requires. "Right now my shipping department is in my living room. It was down here in the shop, but it took up too much space.

"I think we all want to build that one awesome piece of furniture, but we also have to make a living."

"If you didn't have a family, then, sure, you should keep your nose in that dust all day. But my family is very important to me."

Patrick's approach to woodworking is built around the speed and power of commercial-grade equipment. Notice the beefy jointer in the foreground. A lathe stands below the window on the left. Farther back, just beyond the table which supports a run of humidors, is Patrick's Sheng Sheng 37″ wide-belt sander, which is powered by a 20 hp motor. A band saw stands on the right.

The dust from all of his machinery is conducted through flexible hoses and metal conduit to a central dust collection system. Additional air cleansing is achieved via an air filtration system.

"Someday I want to build a three-car garage. That will give me a place to put my shipping department and maybe a space for a spray booth as well."

Maintaining the Business

"If you didn't have a family, then, sure, you should keep your nose in that dust all day. But my family is very important to me."

On a professional level, woodworking isn't something that can be accomplished in 40 short hours a week. Instead it requires enormous investments of time and energy, a principle Patrick knows quite well. "I work seven days a week, eight to ten hours a day, sometimes more. I could start down there at six in the morning and stay down there until one the following morning, and I used to do that, but I don't do it anymore. I never saw my family. It just burned me out. So now I work a fairly normal day, then I leave the shop." He does admit, however, to occasional evening work at his computer.

Patrick sees his shop as a private space, not to be invaded by the casual visitor. In part, this desire was behind his move into this rural area south of Washington, Pennsylvania. "I'm a very private person. My woodworking is very private. Except for my family, the UPS [United Parcel Service] guy is the only person who visits my shop." He shakes his head at the ability of some woodworkers to tolerate interruptions. "I used to buy wood from a fellow here in town, and whenever I'd visit his workshop, he'd have five or ten guys in there sitting around drinking beer. For me this work is too serious and too personal. I couldn't have five or ten buddies in the shop drinking beer and b-s-ing all day. What I do requires a great deal of thought."

Woodworking machinery generates both noise and dust. As a result, many professional woodworkers continually seek to balance the speed and efficiency of machine operations against the cleanliness and quiet of hand-tool operations. Patrick's approach to this problem is, typically for him, very high-tech. "I've got a dust collector with a cyclone. I've got an air cleaner. The cyclone cleans 99.9 percent of the stuff from the air. The bags on my dust collector then clean 99.9 percent of what remains. Then my air cleaner removes 99.9 percent of what the bags miss. So the air is pretty clean.

"And I use an HVLP [high-volume, low-pressure] spray system to minimize overspray. I use water-based finishes. They're nontoxic, and the air cleaner removes most of what's there.

"Even though my equipment does make a lot of noise, I wear hearing protection. And I only work during the day so it doesn't really bother my wife and kids."

Although he does enjoy his time in the shop, he will admit things don't always go quite as planned. "Some days things go well, and some days they don't. I have days when I feel like picking up my boards and throwing them across the room."

Streamlining the Process

"I don't look for perfect technique. That's irrelevant. The end is what's important. Working smarter, not harder."

Although Patrick has a half dozen jigs hanging from his shop wall, he never uses them. "Those are jigs for full-size furniture," he explains. "I don't use them with my boxes. I'm not a jig person. I use another approach." That approach begins with solid design and engineering.

For Patrick, the first consideration is aesthetics. "The most satisfying part of what I do is the design, the art of it. I begin with an idea." Then, after resolving most of the aesthetic issues with the aid of sketches and drawings, he turns to the problem of engineering. "At that point, I ask myself, 'How can I make this piece efficiently enough so that I can sell it to the galleries and still make money?'"

Patrick explains that sometimes he will make changes in the appearance of a piece in order to facilitate efficient construction, but he adds, "Often this improves the appearance of the piece because it results in a cleaner construction." In this context, he points out that the same principles that streamlined the Shaker production processes also streamlined the appearance of Shaker furniture, giving it the graceful simplicity that is now so highly prized.

"That's where the challenge is: How can I sufficiently streamline my processes so that I can make this design at a competitive price? For instance, in the case of my 'Rising Sun' box, my first method for engineering its construction was too complicated. There was no way I could make the piece in that way and sell it for the price I now charge. It had to be reengineered."

This design and engineering process

takes a considerable amount of time. "I'll make a prototype, which may take me three weeks of continuous work. There's a lot of trial and error in the process.

"But I enjoy engineering the pieces and designing them. I like the challenge of figuring out how to make something that's really nice in such a way that I can sell it for half the price I would need to get if I made them one at a time."

Patrick doesn't see himself as a woodworking purist. Sometimes his approach puts him into conflict with firmly entrenched woodworking dogma. "In a production woodshop, you can't do every little detail to perfection. That's where the engineering comes in. I know the limitations of my materials. For example, when I'm gluing something up, I know that I only have to keep a piece in the clamps for 30 minutes, not the 8 hours many woodworkers allow. You can't work the glued-up stock after just 30 minutes, but you can take those clamps off and put them on something else. If the edge was jointed properly, and this is where my machines come into play, there's no stress on that joint and you can remove the clamps."

Another of Patrick's methods involves

The various spring, bar and pipe clamps Patrick uses in his operation are stored on this wall rack between uses.

"I don't look for perfect technique. That's irrelevant. The end is what's important. Working smarter, not harder."

In order to make the most efficient use of space, Patrick's pyramid chests are stacked into a large pyramid between operations.

the concept of the 4-foot board. "Most of my lumber comes in a little over 8 feet in length, so I engineer my pieces to fit within that framework." He points out that many of his pieces have parts measuring a bit less than 24″ or a bit less than 16″ or a bit less than 12″, all of which can be cut from a 48″ length without leaving significant lengths of scrap.

"I also try to work that 4-foot board as much as I can so that I can minimize the handwork later on. I run it through the shaper, through the planer, through the sander—all before I cut the parts to their final dimensions. I try to let that 4-foot board take me most of the way."

Like many other contemporary woodworkers, Patrick eschews the use of classical joinery. There are no hand-cut dovetails on his pieces. In fact there are no dovetails of any kind. Although at one time he put splines in the mitered corners of his boxes, he now uses only biscuits. "They're much stronger in the mitered corners than splines would be.

"I've done the handwork," he ex-

plains. "But I can't afford to take that long to do a job."

Planning Production Runs

"I have everything worked out perfectly in advance: my game plan, how I'm going to do things, how many pieces I'm going to make."

Patrick begins a production run by selecting his lumber. "I like to have a lot of it on hand so I can pick boards that will yield my pieces without leaving a lot of scrap. For example, the pyramids require boards that are 10 inches in width. So when I'm choosing lumber for pyramids, I pick out boards that are 5 or 6 inches wide. I can glue these up for my 10-inch widths without leaving a lot of scrap. There's too much waste when I glue up boards that are 7 inches wide."

When preparing parts for a production run, he prepares many more parts than he will need because he recognizes

> "I have everything worked out perfectly in advance: my game plan, how I'm going to do things, how many pieces I'm going to make."

Patrick's approach to wood-working is emphatically high-tech. He keeps a cellular phone in his back pocket as he works. His business records are kept on this laptop, which he takes to wholesale shows where most of his business is generated.

ITEM SALES DETAIL

	NAME	QUANTITY	SHIP DATE
0996	Pyramid (Lacewood/Maple)		
	Studio Eight	1	8/12/97
	Wood Is Good	1	6/1/97
	Total	2	
0997	Pyramid (Purpleheart/Wenge)		
	The Helen Mitchell Gallery	1	10/15/97
	Total	1	
0999	Pyramid (Oak/Murada)		
	Baker's Gallery	1	10/15/97
	Total	1	
1000	Pyramid (Purpleheart/Maple)		
	The Delicate Touch	5	6/1/97
	The Well	1	9/15/97
	Distinctive Jewelry	2	6/6/97
	Gallery Southwest	3	11/1/97
	Total	11	
	TOTAL	15	

This chart (shown is a brief passage from the nine-page document under which he is currently working) allows Patrick to track his progress in meeting the orders of the galleries he supplies. The descriptive matter to the right of the lot number identifies the product and the combination of woods required in that lot. Directly below that descriptive matter is the name of the gallery that placed the order. Most important is the shipping date on the extreme right of each gallery entry. This date gives Patrick the regular sequence of deadlines for his shop operations.

not every piece built during that run will meet his standards. "A lot of pieces don't make it. I don't try to save every one. Because of a wood defect, a machining error, planer tear-out, some pieces don't measure up. That's where the extras come in."

He does not, however, discard the rejected pieces. "I'll give them to relatives—they're still good pieces—or I'll take them to a retail show and I won't even display them. Then, if somebody comes by and complains about the price, I'll pull out one of these defective pieces and sell it at a discount."

He points to a stack of perhaps 30 pyramids. "I might lose five or ten of those because of one defect or another."

Several times in our conversation, Patrick talks about the importance of finishing what he starts: his home, his shop, a production run. He realizes that it's too easy for a woodworker to start one project while another is waiting to be completed, which can sometimes result in a delay of weeks or even months in the completion of that first project.

He points to the stack of pyramids in one corner of his shop. "I didn't start those until I had those," he points to a gathering of nine bird's-eye maple humidors, "pretty well finished."

Seeing the Beauty of the Machine

While some woodworkers look longingly at the past, at the perceived romance of the eighteenth-century woodworking shop, Patrick has enthusiastically embraced the twentieth century and all that its technology has made available to the professional woodworker. He is as comfortable with a computer keyboard as he is with a hand plane. Instead of a folding carpenter's rule in his back pocket, he carries a cellular phone. When he designs, he doesn't attempt to mimic the look of handwork; instead his designs draw from his rich vocabulary of machine-made shapes, textures and details. Patrick Leonard is prepared for the start of the twenty-first century.

This box, which Patrick identifies as the "Gold Ingot," features figured maple sides.

The growing popularity of cigar smoking has made humidors an important part of Patrick's product line. This particular chest, which can hold 200 cigars, contains a thermometer, a hygrometer and a humidifier.

This distinctive jewelry box reflects Patrick's love of contrasting materials.

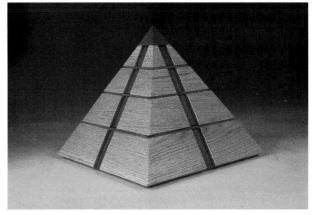

The compartments of this box are accessed by twisting the various levels of the pyramid.

This contemporary chess set takes a modern look at the ancient game. It comes with a set of checkers and storage compartments for the pieces.

CHAPTER THREE

JIM ANDERSON

Maximizing Efficiency

This rocking horse, which he no longer builds, was one of Jim Anderson's first products.

F O C U S : The success of Jim Anderson's product line is based upon three principles: (1) A good jig permits speedy and accurate production; (2) Used industrial-grade machinery offers the production woodshop high performance at relatively low prices; and (3) A large shop permits the easy movement of parts from workstation to workstation.

Spacious. That's the term that best describes Jim Anderson's shop. Or maybe two terms are necessary: *Spacious* and *well equipped.*

It doesn't look like much from the outside. The building needs a little paint. A few weeds have poked through cracks in the concrete parking lot. There's no sign announcing his business to those who drive by. But as Jim later explains, such improvements to the exterior of his business would draw salesmen and casual shoppers, both of whom would interfere with his production work.

I push open the door and enter a room of at least 1000 square feet, well lit, with high ceilings. From an office partitioned off in one corner, Jim Anderson moves forward to greet me. He is fit, trim, maybe 40 years old.

We smile and shake hands. I look around the room. While the outside might appear undernourished, inside, this is a shop any woodworker would envy.

Examining the Shop

Some of the tools in this first room you might find in the shop of any professional woodworker. Dead ahead, there's a Unisaw with a Biesemeyer fence. Standing to the immediate right of the door is a Delta drill press, a machine Jim identifies as having been his first "good" tool. A large homemade stroke sander is pushed up against the back wall. A Powermatic shaper with a 1 hp power feeder stands next to the Delta Unisaw.

Other machines here would look more at home in an industrial setting than in a standard-issue professional shop. Just to the right of the drill press is an ancient but massive Oliver band saw, capable of resawing stock 20″ wide. To the right of

the band saw is an enormous SCM R9 overarm router (a variety imported by Rockwell in the early 1980s). This is a massive machine whose weight is better measured in tons than pounds. Complete with a full set of hydraulics, it's the kind of equipment that the Tim Taylor in all of us dreams of owning. I run my hand covetously over its enormous cast iron table.

We move into the next room, which houses more and even bigger machinery. One piece, a 42″-wide American belt sander powered by a 20 hp motor, is on the way out, having been replaced by a newer and more powerful SCMI model. Along one wall stands a huge multihead horizontal boring machine, a machine capable of drilling thirty-two different mortises at the same time.

Our tour continues. Adjacent to the second room is a small finishing room with a bathroom-sized sheet metal catch basin occupying most of the floor space. Beyond this room is another dedicated to materials storage. Adjacent to that is another room dedicated to the storage of finished products.

Spacious and well equipped. There's even a forklift in the materials-storage room.

Setting Up Life

"You might think that if you work for the government, you're going to be set, but that isn't true."

Like many craftspeople, Jim Anderson took a circuitous route into the woodworking field, stopping along the way to sample several other careers. "I'm a chemist by training. I went to school in Tucson. . . . I was interested in becoming a doctor of psychiatry.

"I got my degree with a double major in chemistry and psychology. I then went to graduate school studying bioenvironmental oceanography in Florida. I

"You might think that if you work for the government, you're going to be set, but that isn't true."

To speed up the finishing process, Jim eliminated brushes, instead relying on dipping many of his products to coat them with the mineral oil finish he uses. Dipped products are then allowed to drain in a shallow sheet metal tank in his finishing room. Here, Jim is dipping the top end of a coatrack.

"The Lord kept bringing jobs to me that required a little more knowledge and maybe one more tool."

thought that might be a nice holding pattern until I could get into medical school. Then I was accepted to the Medical College at the University of Cincinnati. I started there in 1973, and after one semester, I found out I really didn't want to do that."

As Jim explains it, two forces then at work in his life directed him away from his goal of becoming a psychiatrist. "First, I was introduced to the Lord in Florida, and as a result, when I got to medical school, I started evaluating why I wanted to follow that route. I decided that I was more interested in the money than in helping people. Also, I wasn't hitting it off academically in medical school. I think if I'd stayed in, I would have flunked.

"So I went to work at Kettering Labs near Cincinnati working on some projects involving ways to clean up military medical waste water using reverse osmosis so that it would be usable. I was there for six months.

"Then I got a job with the Environmental Protection Agency [EPA], and within three months of the time I started there, they had a reduction in force that wiped out our whole division. Then they

sent me to Denver. I guess that was a kind of indication to me that there isn't a whole lot of security if you trust in men.

"I mentioned that I've given my life to the Lord because I trust in Him, and I can see His provision in everything that's happened to me—how one thing has built on something that happened previously. I can see a step-by-step progression.

"It's not that I would have chosen everything that's happened." Jim shakes his head to emphasize this point. "But all along the way, I can see how He has provided.

"When I went to Denver, I was pretty comfortable with the government work. At that time, I assumed that someday Christ would call me to a mission in, maybe, Africa. So I said to Him, 'Make it real evident when I'm supposed to leave this government job.'

"You know, I was pretty comfortable there. I enjoyed the work. I enjoyed the travel; I worked all over the country. And most of all, I enjoyed the check every other week.

"Then they had a change in administration, and life got real difficult. A bunch of people left my division, and suddenly I was in charge, with a lot of responsibility, and I didn't feel I had adequate training. It got to the point where I hated going to work so bad that I'd get up in the morning and dry heave before I went to work." Jim laughs at the memory. "I had asked the Lord to make it clear when I should leave, and I thought, 'You know, this is pretty evident.' "

By the time his EPA job had begun to wear on him emotionally, other parts of Jim's life had combined to offer him enough security to make a change of jobs a possibility. "I was newly married. We had a house in Denver. My wife had a decent job, and we didn't have any children.

"At about that time, the man who had

been my boss at the EPA had left his job and was in the process of buying a chain of doughnut shops in the Denver area. He offered me a job as manager of those doughnut shops, and I thought this was a way out."

Spurred by the promise of a job managing doughnut shops, Jim left the EPA and the security of government employment. "But that doughnut shop thing never panned out."

Setting Up Shop

"The Lord kept bringing jobs to me that required a little more knowledge and maybe one more tool."

Jim's background made the manual trades an obvious consideration at this point in his life. "As a child I had seen my father work for himself. He had a business installing those big underground tanks at gas stations. He then built houses. Then he bought a Laundromat. I saw a lifetime of self-employment.

"I also had an interest, since a seventh-grade shop class, in woodworking. So when I quit the government job, I took a look at my tool kit. I had a hammer, a saw, some miscellaneous hand tools, and I said to myself, 'I can do something with these to make some money.'

"My wife Jackie's boss had a husband who didn't do much around the house. She [Jackie's boss] said, 'Why don't you go into a home repair business? Some women are single. Others have husbands who aren't into home repair. Women need someone who can come out and install a light switch, fix a faucet.' She said, 'You can't get people to come out and do things like that.'

"She hired me to build a fence. I didn't make much money at it because I needed another tool, but that's another sign of the progression. It seems to me that the Lord brought to me jobs that I could do, each time requiring just a little more tooling and a little more knowledge.

"I did everything. I did repair of aluminum gutters, which is miserable work. I did staircases. I did drywall. I did plumbing. For two years, I worked this way. I took on all kinds of work, learning new stuff, buying new tools.

"I never charged enough. Sometimes I lost money on jobs. But I kept on." Then, in the space of three weeks, after two years of thoroughly satisfied customers, Jim did work for two different individuals who thought he'd cheated them on his labor charges. "And here I was cheating myself. If I worked 40 hours, I charged them for 30, working for about three dollars an hour.

"It was frustrating, but I think the Lord sent me those two people for a reason, because that's what finally convinced me to look at another way to make a living."

"In 1980, after two years of not making any money, I decided to come up with a product."

"At that time, we had a little one-car garage that I'd turned into a shop. What I wanted was a product that I could make in that shop and sell to stores.

> "In 1980, after two years of not making any money, I decided to come up with a product."

The manufacture of wooden heads for street sweeper brushes is an important part of Jim's business. Here, Jim is stacking completed heads. These are made of a special 9-ply material designed to be resistant to water and to collisions with curbs.

"While looking around the stores for products, I saw a pine rocking horse with a little glass eye. It was made by a company called Woods of America. The Denver, a chain of stores in Colorado, was selling these horses for $125.

"I saw them, and I thought I could make them. I thought I could make a better horse and sell it for less. My wife's brother, Pete, who has a degree in art from Bowling Green State University, was staying with us at the time. So he and I got together and worked out a design.

"When I got my first horse built, when I'd refined the design, I called The Denver. I got a purchasing agent on the phone. I described the rocking horse I'd made, and she said, 'I think we might be interested in your product.' So I asked her how many she wanted, and she said, 'We might take three to five hundred.'

"Now, they didn't take that many. They actually ordered about 120. But they did order, and I thought, 'Wow. I'm in business.'"

Success, however, didn't come so easily. Suddenly, there were problems that Jim had to solve very quickly. The first was space for manufacturing. While his

one-car garage was big enough for small-scale shop work, it wasn't nearly large enough for an operation that would create more than 100 rocking horses.

Fortunately, however, a solution was at hand. In addition to the one-car garage where he had been working, Jim and Jackie had a two-car garage into which Jim decided to move his business. "I built a workbench and ran 220 [volts] out to the building."

Then, having solved the shop-space problem, Jim turned his attention to another concern. "I had given the store a price on these rocking horses of $55. That was boxed and delivered for $55, and I hadn't looked into packaging. I just made some assumptions which didn't turn out to be accurate. When I went to get prices on boxes, I found that each one was going to cost me five or six dollars."

He decided, then, to make his own boxes. "I figured out how to make them. I thought for as many as I needed I could build myself a box-making table with all the stops and everything on it. I found I could make the boxes for $1.10 [each]. So I went to a cardboard factory and picked up a truckload of cardboard cut to the right size.

"I got a hot-melt glue gun to fasten the boxes together. I had labels printed up with the company logo on them. It was all very professional. That has always been important to me. I wanted to look professional.

"Then Jackie's boss came back from a trip somewhere, and she had an idea for another product. She said, 'You need to make a coatrack.' She said, 'I saw the cutest little coatrack. It was painted white with this animal head on top of it.'

"At that time, we belonged to some woodworking guilds, and these guilds sponsored craft shows. Well, when my wife's boss came back with this idea for a coatrack, we decided that since the

Jim Anderson shows some of the products that he sells at retail shows. The trays stacked in the background are among his more popular items. Many are made of figured and contrasting woods.

Denver Broncos were so big in the area, we would build a coatrack with the Broncos colors on it and then we would try to sell it at the guilds' shows."

The coatracks did sell, but not well enough and not for a high enough price. However, the rocking horse was continuing to sell—The May Co. had placed an order—and Jim was sufficiently encouraged to consider investing some money into his business. "After that first year, after selling a hundred rocking horses, I decided to add a little equipment.

"What I was thinking is this: If I'd sold over a hundred rocking horses to The Denver and then a number of others to the May Co., maybe I could expand my business to reach other parts of the country."

In this regard, Jim considered an idea put forth by the buyer at the May Co. "He suggested that we go to the Toy Fair that's held in New York City every February. I sent to the Toy Fair and got a great big thick book of people who buy there, page after page of businesses looking to buy toys for their retail stores. And I thought, 'Man, alive. If I sold to even a

fraction of the businesses listed there, I'd have a major business just making rocking horses.'

"We had an old, beat-up trailer we'd bought at an auction somewhere. We packed up our samples. We made a display booth and went to the show.

"The show cost us $2000 just to get in. Plus we had all the other expenses: hotel, food, travel. I think we probably sold enough rocking horses to pay for our trip. Some went to a store headquartered up in Vermont: The Wooden Soldier. We also got our horse in a catalog put out by one of the branches of Neiman-Marcus, the Horchow Collection."

Building the Business

"Somebody would come to me with a job, and I'd spend all the money I made on that job on a new piece of equipment. I was always reinvesting."

Reinvestment is one recurring theme in Jim's story. When he began to earn money working with his hands, he

> "Somebody would come to me with a job, and I'd spend all the money I made on that job on a new piece of equipment. I was always reinvesting."

Jim's new **SCMI 43″** sander is nearly ready to be put into operation.

Jim uses this **SCM R9** overarm router to drill bristle mortises in the wooden heads of street sweeper brushes.

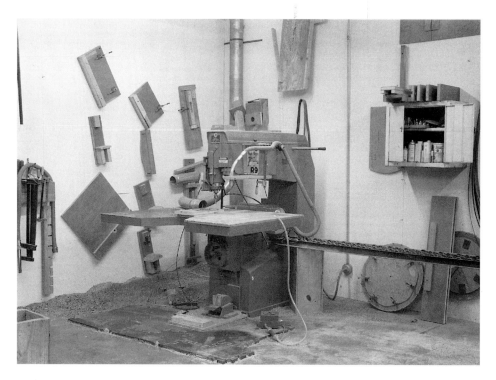

acknowledged that a good portion of his income would have to be reinvested into his business, specifically and primarily into new tools. This approach has been characteristic of his career at every step ever since.

When he moved to Carey, Ohio, after his initial successes as a toy maker, he reinvested the money he and and Jackie had made through the sale of their house into a building in downtown Carey that could double as a residence and a shop. There were a number of upstairs apartments and a shop and several first-floor commercial sites. Then, as that building began to fill up with businesses needing downtown locations, Jim bought a large building—his current shop—just outside Carey and converted it to serve the needs of his rapidly growing production business, adding equipment as his finances permitted.

By purchasing new tools, Jim has improved the capabilities of his shop, allowing him to take on new accounts. For example, today, one-quarter of his year is spent making wooden brush heads for a company that supplies completed

brushes for street-sweeping machines. Jim's continued investment in ever larger shops and ever more powerful equipment enabled him to service this account.

This notion of reinvestment applies not only to capital improvements but also to marketing. "During our first year, we signed up for almost 20 shows, and at most of them we lost money. It rained all that summer, and I'll bet I lost money on 18 of the 20 shows I did that year.

"During those 18 bad shows, I'd sit in the rain and talk to those other exhibitors about what shows were good to do. That was where I first started to hear stories about the Yankee Peddler Festival [an enormous outdoor arts-and-crafts show held just south of Cleveland, Ohio, on three consecutive weekends]. Now I have three or four shows I do every year. I know some good promoters, and when they put on a show, I try and do them.

"I've heard people complaining about the Yankee Peddler promoters and all their rules. But the way I look at it is: I'm not a show promoter. These people obviously know what they're doing. So I'm not going to complain about how they run things. If they want me to throw my trash away, I'll do that. If they want me to eat my trash, I'll do that."

This antique Oliver band saw has a 20″ resaw capacity.

Maximizing Efficiency

At every step in his woodworking career, Jim Anderson has searched for more efficient methods of work. To avoid the stifling effects of a cramped work environment, he moved his shop from a one-car garage to a two-car garage, then later to a large commercial building in downtown Carey, then later still into its present spacious quarters outside the city. When facing the expense of custom-made shipping boxes for his rocking horses, he designed not only a box but also a table, with stops, on which the box could be rapidly produced in sufficient quantities. Today, if a shop operation be-gins to drag and reduce shop profits, Jim designs jigs and fixtures to accelerate the production process. In many cases, he not only improves the process, he also improves the quality of the finished product.

Buying Machinery

On the day I arrive to speak with Jim about his operation, he is hooking up a huge, and new (to him), wide-belt sander with a 43″ capacity, driven by a 30 hp motor. Scattered across the room are sections of heavy cable, switches, junction boxes and an electric motor he will use to feed stock into the machine. More parts—all large, heavy, painted—rest on a large, open-bed trailer sitting in the next room.

Jim explains that he bought the used machine at an auction and he's never seen it in operation. "I buy all my equipment at auctions. I've never had a lot of money, so I've had to wait for good buys." Jim shakes his head. "It's just incredible how things have worked out. Whenever I've needed something, it's been there."

He points to another machine in the same room, this one resting now in front of an overhead door. "This new sander will replace that old one." The old machine has the look of a Victorian antique. Lacking the stamped-metal sleekness of the new SCMI, the old machine is assembled of large iron parts cast into the baroque shapes of a piece of modern sculpture. Jim assures me this older machine, which still works, has provided him with years of solid service.

Jim Anderson Solves a Problem

Several of the hall trees in Jim's product line use as coat hooks 4″-long dowels capped with small turned wooden balls. The balls are purchased turned and sanded from a supplier. Jim cuts a mortise into each ball to receive the end of the dowel. The dowels are then glued into place in those mortises, after which the other ends of the dowels are glued into mortises cut into the hall tree's post.

The trickiest part of this operation is boring a ¾″ mortise into the spherical surface of each 1¼″ ball. Conventional clamping caused enough pressure on the ball to distort its shape. A round mortise drilled into a pressure-distorted ball resulted in a mortise that was noticeably oblong when the clamping pressure was relieved. To solve this problem (and to make the process of drilling these mortises more efficient), Jim designed a jig which uses a vacuum to hold the ball in place during the mortising process.

PHOTO 1. This photo shows the completed jig, which is clamped to the edge of the drill press table. An operator sits in the chair, controlling the vacuum clamp with the foot switch on the floor. Mortised balls are dropped into the section of galvanized ductwork, from which they fall into the box at the lower right.

PHOTO 2. The ball in this photo is resting in a hole bored into the surface of the 2×4 which forms the body of the jig and is held there by vacuum pressure. When the pressure is released, the bit is raised from the mortise. The ledge through which the bit passes knocks any stuck balls from the bit when the bit is raised. The ball is then dropped into the ductwork section.

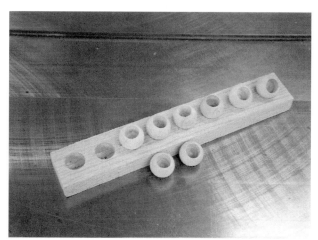

PHOTO 3. A jig doesn't need to be complicated in order to be useful. This I×2 strip of oak is drilled with a row of shallow mortises, each of which provides a nesting iplace where the mortised balls can be secured while glue is swabbed into the mortises.

These kitchen accessories—cutting boards, hot pad, lazy Susan—are typical of the offerings of the Anderson Company.

These trays and their accompanying stands are some of Jim's bread-and-butter items.

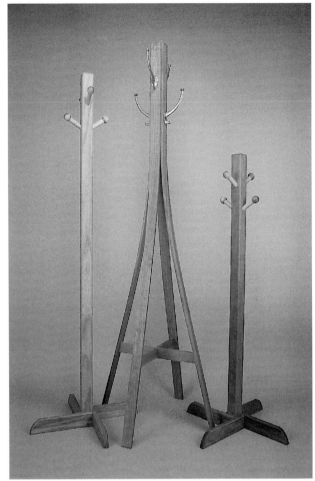

Jim offers a variety of coatracks. These particular models are made of cherry.

Jim offers this recipe box in a number of different woods, including some which retain natural knotholes.

CHAPTER FOUR

RAY MUNIAK

The Sum of My Experiences

In addition to a line of jewelry, each year Ray also does a number of large, framed works, like this portrait of a flying eagle.

F O C U S : In addition to large, framed pieces, Ray Muniak produces scores of earrings, pendants and brooches, all using a series of cutting, sculpting and assembly techniques he has developed over the last 15 years. These techniques are built on three principles: (1) 15-mil plastic makes sturdy cutting templates; (2) Double-sided tape permits parts to be stacked prior to sawing; and (3) Work sticks make it possible to hold the tiniest parts so they can be shaped and sanded.

I first see Ray Muniak's work in mid-September at Yankee Peddler. It is raining. It has been raining all day, and I'm tired. The exit gate is just ahead, and I'm anxious to get back to the dry and familiar comfort of my car. Then, out of the corner of my eye, I see something unusual hanging from the upper levels of a nearby booth. I look more closely and see a framed assembly of small, sculpted pieces of some very pale wood. At first glance, my eye doesn't read the imagery. All I see is a pleasing arrangement of shapes. Then, as I come nearer, I realize I'm looking at flowers.

My eyes move to other work hanging from the booth, and I see more natural imagery—trees, animals, vegetation—executed in bits of naturally finished woods. I see walnut, poplar, pink ivorywood.

Intarsia? Am I looking at intarsia? That's what the work most closely resembles, but it is different than any intarsia I've seen. Instead of a single layer of tightly fit and sculpted bits of wood, this work is executed in many layers, with foregrounds moved aggressively toward the viewer.

I move through the crowd in the direction of the booth. There, just below eye level, I see jewelry cases filled with earrings, pendants, brooches. Again, the imagery is straight from nature. Again, the pieces are created from bits of sculpted and naturally finished wood.

Examining the Shop

Fast-forward to November. The temperature is in the low 30s, and snowflakes the size of breath mints tumble from the gray sky.

The large A-frame that houses both Ray Muniak's home and gallery is tucked

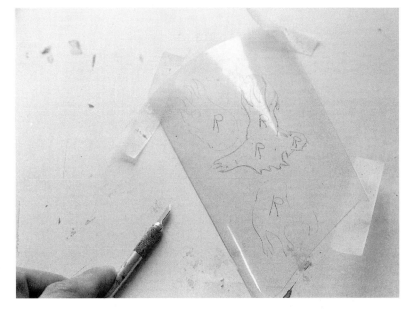

comfortably into place among the rolling hills and hardwood forests south of Cleveland, Ohio. A stand of pine trees with neatly trimmed skirts edges close to one side of the long driveway. A picnic table sits in the middle of that stand, perhaps a hundred yards from Ray's front door, its feet resting on an inches-thick blanket of brown needles. Although there is snow on the yard immediately against the house, no snow has penetrated the canopy of pine boughs.

No one answers my knock on the

His jewelry-making process begins by cutting patterns from 15-mil sheets of plastic.

He outlines in red those cuts marking edges that must abut the edges of other parts. The red lines act as reminders that these cuts must be particularly accurate.

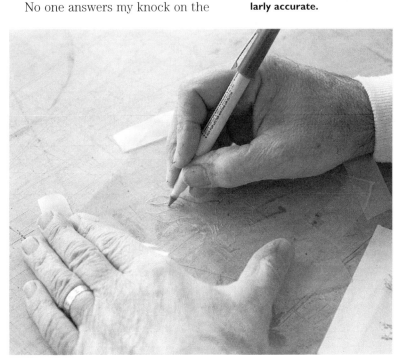

He resaws using inexpensive, thin-rim blades he buys from Sears.

gallery door. I peer through the glass. Ray's intarsia-like pictures hang from the walls.

I notice another door opening into the A-frame's second floor from the deck above my head. I climb the stairs and knock. Through the sliding glass door, I see a slender woman talking on the phone. She smiles, puts down the phone and invites me in.

As we talk, Ray appears. Like his wife, he is slender. He wears a sweatshirt and jeans. His handshake is firm.

First, we go downstairs to the gallery. The lighting is indirect, hushed. On every wall of the main room there are five or six meticulously executed scenes from nature, each created from bits of carefully arranged, naturally finished woods.

There is another room in which Ray displays wooden jewelry similar to the pieces I noticed at Yankee Peddler two months earlier. Although there are many different images in his collection, Ray makes multiple copies of designs he knows will sell well. He shows me a dozen jewelry pins, each adorned with a tiny elephant sculpted from a bit of pale wood.

His studio occupies a two-story barn behind the house/gallery. On the first floor, he has a spray booth and an area for materials storage.

The second floor, where he actually assembles his work, is divided into two rooms. One, which he identifies as the "dirty room," houses his woodworking machinery: table saw, drill press, thickness planer, band saw and a variety of stationary sanding machines. Surprisingly, all are modest priced. I see none of the top-of-the-line equipment usually found in the shops of woodworking professionals.

A string of Christmas lights is hung along the room's back wall. Ray explains that they are set up to flicker when his phone rings so he'll be aware of calls even if machinery is running.

Ray identifies the other second-floor room as his "clean room." Inside there is an enormous worktable, the base of which is occupied by a number of huge drawers. A counter runs along one end and one side providing additional work space. Above the counter at the end of the room is a series a large windows overlooking Ray's home, his yard and the rolling, wooded hills beyond.

Tracing His Roots

"As a patternmaker, I could make almost anything out of wood. That was great training."

Ray traces the roots of his distinctive approach to woodworking back to his childhood. "When I was eight or nine years old, I fell in love with puzzles. I just loved putting puzzles together. I remember my dad taking me to rummage shops, and we'd buy these puzzles, and they would drive me crazy because there were always one or two pieces missing."

These childhood experiences with puzzles not only stimulated Ray's interest in creating imagery from the assembly of small parts, they also encouraged him to think about color. "People may not realize it, but when you do puzzles, it trains you in color."

> "As a patternmaker, I could make almost anything out of wood. That was great training."

His interest in woodworking was spurred by his father. "I started to appreciate woodworking because I would watch my dad. He was a metal-pattern maker, and at home, he would make kitchen cabinets and furniture for the house. And I just loved watching him work.

"And of course, as a little kid, I tried to do what he did. But, you know, I might take a half hour to cut a 2×4."

As a teenager, Ray first tried woodworking on his own, starting with simple projects. Then, by the time he'd reached high school, he was building more and more complex pieces, the most challenging of which was a cedar chest he built when he was 16 or 17.

Ray attended St. Ignatius High School in Cleveland, a school long noted for its athletic teams and its success at preparing students for higher education. "I planned to go to college, but after two years they [his high school] kicked me out. I think they knew I wasn't college material. I wanted to work with my hands. So I went to West Tech, a trade school, and I became a wood-pattern maker.

"I then got a job with a good company, Cleveland Standard Pattern, where there was a great variety of things to do. A lot of pattern shops tend to be specialized in certain areas, but the company that I worked with, we worked with plastics, with metal, with plaster, with different kinds of material. Sizewise, we did anything from the size of a portable tape recorder to the size of a Buick."

Turning was an important skill in this shop, and Ray found this discipline almost irresistible. "For a while, I got hooked on wood turning. In this particular shop, there was a woodturner who had been there for 60, 65 years. He was, I think, about 85 years old. He retired while I was serving my apprenticeship. I finished my five-year apprenticeship in 1966, and I took over the turning."

During his tenure in this first pattern

Ray feeds material past the thin-rim blade on his table saw.

shop, Ray met and married his first wife, and he began working with wood in order to equip his home with necessary items. "I was making a lot of things around the home—toys, furniture, decks, things like that—but low-end. I had four kids, so there wasn't much money.

"I worked at that first pattern shop until 1968. Then I left that company and went to different company where I made patterns up to 1970.

"That was a tough time. There was a little bit of a recession, and I was out of work. We had just built a house. My wife had just had our fourth baby. So I was fiddling around, refinishing furniture, things like that. And I saw an ad in the paper for a job in a cabinet shop, Nagle Manufacturing, and they hired me. And after three months, I was getting journeyman's wages in a different trade.

"It was a great shop. They did all kinds of work. They might do a cupola for a church or all the woodwork for an expensive dress shop. Once I made a set of doors for Cleveland Heights High School from red oak, 8′ tall, each 4′ wide, frame and panel. I made six or eight of those doors.

"I worked at Nagle for two or three years. At about that time, I saw an ad for a part-time job in a pattern shop evenings, Saturdays. Later, I got tired of working in the cabinet shop so I went to work at the pattern shop, the Bukach Pattern shop, full-time. Their work was more specialized; they focused on smaller things. I remember spending almost two months working on the fuel injector for an airplane, and it [the injector] was no bigger than my fist. The pattern was made of mahogany. In this particular case, I worked through the whole process. I was both a wood- and a metal-pattern maker.

"At one of the pattern shops I worked at, I picked up an idea that I still use. In fact, it's one of the most important materials I use in my shortcuts here now: a 15-mil sheet plastic for my templates. Also, at that shop, we used something else that's very important to my methods today: double-faced tape. And these are things that maybe I never would have thought of if I hadn't worked in that shop."

Although he enjoyed his work in the pattern shops, some of his most interesting woodwork was done on his own, outside the shops. Ray remembers one particular customer who provided him with an opportunity to do some of the most challenging woodwork of his career.

"Back in 1975, I got hooked up with someone who wanted some high-end furniture. She had a beautiful home in Pepper Pike designed by Frank Lloyd Wright, and she wanted some special furniture for the home.

"She would say, 'Well, I want a coffee table.' But she didn't want just a coffee table; she wanted a piece of art. So I worked with her decorator to choose woods that would look right: pecan, walnut, woods with great figure. I did about fifteen pieces of furniture for this woman in Pepper Pike.

"Then I went to work at a plastic-vacuum-forming company, Aurora National. There, I designed and made all its tooling, starting from wood models, going all the way to the final aluminum castings."

Building the Business

"The only art class I've ever taken is art history in college. In fact, that's the only class I ever took in college. And I got an A in that class, which means I have a 4.0 average in college."

Although his apprenticeship in the first pattern shop equipped Ray with the technical skills needed to create almost anything from wood, as an artist he is largely self-taught, relying on chance and intuition to supply him with the ideas that distinguish his work from that of other craftspeople working with images created from bits of wood.

The first of these ideas, the result of chance, came to Ray in 1981 while on a trip to San Francisco with his wife and children.

"We went to a place called Pier 54, which was very close to Fisherman's Wharf. It was a high-end shopping area, filled with little shops. My wife and I went into this one restaurant, and I'm sitting there having a beer. And I look up on the wall, and there's a piece of what is now called *lath art*, made by a company called Degroot. At that time they were making things exclusively for places on the West Coast and the East Coast.

"This piece showed a boat in the water. There were waves. There was a sky. It was made of lath going in all these different directions. You still see this kind of work today, in the Ground Rounds and the Ponderosas [restaurants] of the world.

"I looked at that piece, and I said to my wife, 'I'm going to do that.' And about a month later, I did one. I put it together, and my sister Dorothy, who's an artist, came by and encouraged me.

"I then paged through some magazines and found a picture in *Bon Appetit* magazine with that design." He points at a piece of lath art hanging on the wall behind us. The piece, showing a land-scape of egrets, rushes and sky, is composed of small pieces of lath, each one cut to fit and painted: green for vegetation, blue for sky. Although the image has a stiffness uncharacteristic of his current work, this piece already exhibits the layering that separates his work from the now familiar lath art. Details of the middle ground and foreground are set in place on top of the background layer, a practice that gives the image the 3-D look of a stereopticon scene.

"I then did a series of scenes from Rousseau's [French primitive painter of scenes from nature] paintings. At that time I was doing jigsaw cuts. Everything, in every layer, had to come together, and then you just put this jigsaw puzzle together. That was 1981."

For two or three years, Ray worked in that manner, using paint to supply color to his completed scenes. Then chance stepped in once again, supplying Ray with an idea that ultimately became one of the dominant themes in his work. "Someone came to me and said, 'Why don't you do a scene like that but use natural woods?'

"Now this was before I'd heard of Judy Gale Roberts. This is what she does.

"Up to that time, I'd been using painted western cedar—nice and light, easy to sand, very stable. It also has a variety of natural colors. So I took some of that cedar and made a piece with natural colors. It was a very contemporary piece—a man, and a woman in a big flowing hat—and it was well received, so I made a couple like that.

"Then one day I'm thinking in my shop and I noticed some of the woods I had lying around. I said, 'Hey, I've got some poplar, and it's green. I've got some mahogany, and it's red. Pine's white, and I've got other stuff.'"

This idea, perhaps more than any other, has given Ray's work it's particular

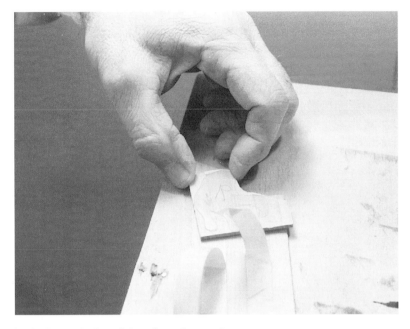

After a section long enough for the part being cut is removed from the stock, that section and its plastic pattern are oriented on the remaining stock. Notice that the paper backing strips on the double-faced tape have been pulled back just far enough to fasten this section to the remaining stock.

look. Instead of applying the color to the bits of wood, he now searches for a piece whose natural color and figure permit him to best tell the story he wants to tell. "So my methods evolved. When I started, everything was done flat, in one layer, in quarter-inch material. Now, it's very different."

Selling the Artwork

"At that moment, it hit me: Wow, I can make some money at this!"

"In 1983, I started to sell a few pieces. Very early on I had some shows here in Cleveland, downtown in a place called the Arcade. I had a show there and somebody liked my work. I put my stuff in a gallery there. Of course, nothing ever sold. One piece was marked $3000. Another was marked $5000. But," Ray shrugs, "these big scenes would take me forever. I was taking months to assemble a single piece. Now, I can do pieces like that in a couple of weeks.

"I started having these little parties at my shows. I would invite family and friends. We would have cheese and crackers. We'd drink wine, and we'd have

"At that moment, it hit me: Wow, I can make some money at this!"

this good old time. And I might be written up in the paper, and it was fun.

"And then in 1983 a Ukrainian man from the area, who had this international gallery, saw my work. His name was Yerema Harabatch. He came by one day and said, 'I want to be your agent.'

"He then made up this pamphlet of all these artists. I had a picture in there, and he distributed this thing all over the world. He managed to get one of my pieces in a gallery in the Flats [an area of downtown Cleveland near the Rock and Roll Hall of Fame], and it did sell. In fact it sold for $1000. The problem was Yerema Harabatch took 30 percent, and the gallery took 30 percent. I ended up with a check for $490.

"So a year or two later, I ran into him and he said, 'Why don't we do a show? Your work is progressing nicely.'

"Again, I got the wine. I got the cheese, got the crackers, all that stuff. So we're having the show. My family's there. My friends are there. My kids are there. I'm having a good old time.

"Then I look and there are these red dots starting to show up. I think, 'What are these red dots?' So I went up to the gallery owner and asked, and he looks at me and

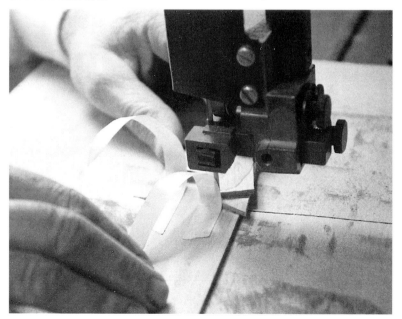

Another section is being cut off on the band saw.

says, 'You dunce. Those mean sales.'

"This is 1985. Then about a year later I got another break. Baldwin-Wallace College runs a very nice summer theater there that's gone on for years and years. One of the people I worked with at the last pattern shop also worked at the theater part-time, and she said, 'You know, I think I can get some of your stuff on the walls there at the summer theater.' So I went to meet the guy, and we set it up. But I don't think I sold anything at all the first year. But the second year, I sold a ton of stuff.

"At that time, I was still working at that fourth pattern shop, but I wasn't working a full 40 hours a week on shop stuff. I think I was down to about 32 hours a week on that. The rest of my time I spent on my artwork.

"Then one day, the boss called me into the office and said, 'I'm going to have to let you go.'" In Ray's view, the firing was motivated by his boss's jealousy of the success Ray was having with his artwork. Although at first angry about being fired, Ray quickly saw the firing from a new perspective.

"I think it was the best thing that ever happened to me. He kicked me out, so my wife and I talked and looked at our expenses. We decided we could could make it for three months. So I went into art full-time."

One of the first (and most effective) promotional tools Ray employed was an unmanned kiosk at Cleveland Hopkins Airport. It stood in the airport concourse, visible to travelers coming into and going out of Cleveland. On it, Ray displayed samples of his work, along with paper and pen so that interested parties could leave their phone numbers. Ray then contacted these individuals, a practice which led to many sales.

"Even with all those people moving through the airport, I got, on average, only one contact per day." Ray shrugs and adds, "But it worked. They were the right contacts."

Occasionally, Ray did open houses at that time. "Invitations were sent to people whose names were gleaned from lists generated by these feeder things, like the airport kiosk. People would come, and I would serve chocolate chip cookies and wine and crackers. Together with the sales I got out of the kiosk, I kind of made it. I was making some money. It was alright.

"Maybe a year later I stopped doing the kiosk. We saved $600 a month there, and we put the money into other kinds of advertising. I began sending out hundreds of postcards."

Although his list of clients has grown steadily, Ray has found that people rarely come to his open houses without first having seen his work somewhere, whether at the airport kiosk or at retail shows like Yankee Peddler. "There aren't a lot of word-of-mouth sales. I would guess that 95 percent of my sales result from someone looking at my work first-hand. Typically, people return again and again, buying one piece, then another."

Like many contemporary crafts-people, Ray has experimented with a number of different strategies for getting his work out in front of the public, although most have failed to generate much business. "I have handed out hundreds of business cards, but, to this day, I don't think I have made one sale as a result of business cards. And I had a brochure, although I'm not even sure I ever recovered printing costs."

Ray has experienced mixed results at retail shows. He has, in fact, been turned down by several. "It's just the truth about arts-and-crafts shows. You can have the best work in the world and still get turned down. Part of that is bad slides, but I also think it's politics. People know somebody—maybe they have a cousin who does woodworking—so they get in, and you don't.

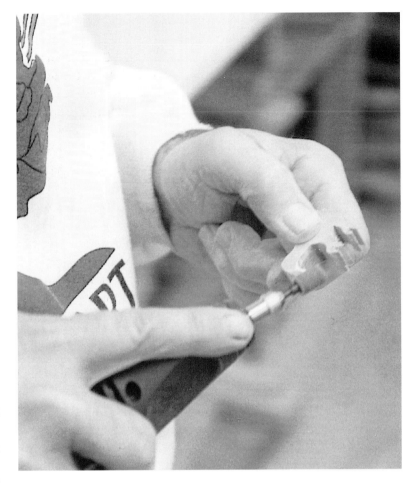

With a Dremel tool, Ray cleans up band saw marks.

"Also, there are some strange things happening in the arts-and-crafts shows. I remember going to an area show after having been turned down by the jury. I went up to this marquetrist. I put my finger up on his signature on one of the pieces, and I noticed it was real rough. What he had done was buy the artwork from someone else. Then he burned his name onto it.

"Much of the work you now see at craft shows is manufactured by the millions, out of Korea. I was at a show once where we had this problem. Someone came up to me and said, 'Do you know what's going on? Go around to the back and you'll see that they have custom-made boxes, with computer strips identifying each box. They tear open these sealed boxes, and they're selling out of the boxes.'

"When I looked at the goods, I saw that the tole painting on one piece was

"One of the most difficult parts of this is the engineering. You've got to be able to put something together that has structural integrity."

Tiny parts are fastened to the work stick with brads. This allows them to be held securely as they are being sculpted and sanded.

exactly like the tole painting on the next. And," the anger is clear in Ray's voice, "they won Best of Show."

Ray hasn't confined his marketing efforts to a single segment of the population. One current area of emphasis for his sales approach is the corporate customer. "Right now my biggest customer is the Davey Tree Company. They're the tree surgeon company. They do a lot of work for power companies, trimming trees back from the power lines. Davey's the biggest. I made contact with Davey Tree Company through my kiosk at Cleveland Hopkins."

Planning Production

"One of the most difficult parts of this is the engineering. You've got to

be able to put something together that has structural integrity."

On the day that I visited Ray, he was preparing to make a run of eagle pins to be sold by an area high school booster club as a fund-raiser. Ray permitted me to follow him through this process.

Good design reflects more than the craftsperson's aesthetic sensibilities. It also reflects the economic realities of the marketplace. Ray recognizes that there is a price ceiling for the various items of wooden jewelry he offers for sale. "You have to design so that it's simple to keep the cost down. They [booster club customers] only want to pay 15 or 20 dollars for these things, so you have to plan it so that you can make four or five of these in one hour."

His designs begin on paper. Then, once the details and proportions have been laid out, he transfers them to clear 15-mil plastic and cuts out the various patterns with a craft knife. This is a procedure that he follows both for his large framed pieces and for his wooden jewelry. "One of the best parts about this plastic is that it leaves a white edge after it's been cut." This white edge is a very visible line Ray can follow at the band saw.

Although he often makes use of tropical woods, for some pieces he uses only domestics. The many drawers in his clean room are filled with a rainbow of woods originating in countries all over the world.

Once he has selected material of the proper size, color and figure, Ray resaws that material on a table saw using a cheap, thin-rim blade he found at Sears. He then moves to the thickness planer and dresses the stock to a thickness of ¼", a dimension that has become a standard for his methods. "I used to sand the surfaces when I was assembling pieces from flat stock, but now that I sculpt everything, I don't have to sand. I just work with planed material."

Once his patterns have been cut and

his stock has been properly thicknessed, Ray begins to lay out his band saw cuts. Double-faced tape is the key to this process in Ray's shop. "Double-faced tape is the savior when I'm making multiple copies."

He begins by running a couple lengths of double-faced tape along his stock, leaving the paper backing on the top surface. (This backing will be removed in increments as he lays out more copies of this part.) He then orients one of the plastic templates on a length of thicknessed stock. Correct placement is very important. "You have to worry about grain. On this particular piece, there are little feet. So when you're placing the plastic template on the wood, you have to make sure the template is positioned so that the grain won't run across the feet. You need to look at the piece and decide, 'Which is the part that's delicate? Which is the part that's likely to break off?'

"In other cases, where you don't have things that are likely to break off, you're not worried about strength. You're concerned about beauty. Which way does the grain look the best?"

Conservation of material is another consideration. "Particularly when you're using woods of cost, you want to make the most efficient use of your material."

Once he has decided on the proper orientation, he moves to the band saw to cut off enough length for that part. He then pulls back the paper backing strip on the top side of the double-faced tape—just enough to allow him to fasten the cutoff to the top of the next section of the stock. This process is repeated until he has a stack of chips all held together with double-faced tape.

Band sawing this stack to the correct profile is the next step. Surprisingly, Ray uses a very dull ⅛" band saw blade to do this finicky cutting. He explains, "When the blade is dull, it doesn't cut so quickly. I have more control."

After he has profiled this stack of parts, he sculpts the top surface of the top piece with a Dremel tool, then removes it from the stack, after which he sculpts the top surface of the next piece.

At this point, he bores a very tiny hole in each part on the drill press. This hole will ultimately be used in mounting the pin to its metal backing. At this time, however, the hole will be used to affix the tiny part to a work stick. This is done by driving a tiny brad through the hole and into the soft wood of the work stick. One by one, each of the stacked parts is mounted in this manner.

Then, by holding the work stick in his hand (or in a vise), Ray can do any additional sculpting or sanding that may be necessary without fumbling to hold the tiny part in his fingers.

The Sum of My Experience

"People are always asking me how they can make what I make. You know what I tell them? I tell them if their grandfather didn't have red hair, they can't make what I make." Ray laughs. "Because everything I do is a result of every experience I've had. If my father hadn't worked with wood, I might not have gotten into woodworking. If I hadn't been a patternmaker for 15 years, I would work differently. If I hadn't seen that first piece of lath art in San Francisco, I wouldn't be doing what I am today. This work," Ray gestures at the shop around him, "is the sum of every bit of my life.

"What I tell people when they ask me that question is that they shouldn't try to make what I make; they should make what *they* make."

These flower and animal portraits are typical of the images Ray uses in his line of wooden jewelry.

This image, which Ray has named *World Tree*, is assembled from bits of wood originating in countries from around the globe.

CHAPTER FIVE

Doing What They Love

The raised bed of this mini dump truck reveals the dumping mechanism.

FOCUS: With the assistance of his wife, Carole, Ed Schmidt uses production runs to manufacture hundreds of high-quality toys each year. They sell these toys at retail shows and through a handsomely printed catalog.

The Schmidts' success is built on four principles: (1) It's cheaper to buy certain key components—wheels and dowel stock, for example—than it is to make them; (2) Expensive equipment pays for itself in terms of reduced labor costs; (3) Sharp detailing—figured and contrasting woods, laser etching, smooth finish—gives a toy enormous curb appeal; and (4) Craftspeople should do what they love.

When the road switches from pavement to gravel to dirt, I realize that I've missed the driveway of Ed and Carole Schmidt's home on the east side of Columbus, Ohio. In a grove of hardwoods stripped to the bone by December winds, I back and fill, turning my car around. Then, watching closely on my second pass down the road, I find the address.

Their home is a comfortable two-story with a deep front yard bordered on one side by a narrow asphalt driveway. I follow that driveway to its terminus in a large parking area behind the house. At the back of that parking area is a building that might once have been a garage but now, having had its width and depth increased by additions, more closely resembles a small manufacturing plant.

When I knock at the back door of the house, Ed answers with a smile and an offered hand. Carole is inside waiting in the family room. We sit down to talk.

Getting Started in Woodworking

"Carole showed me some magazines. 'Here,' she said. 'Look at these wood items. Are you interested in these?'"

Ed got involved in craft work because of his wife. Ed explains, "Twenty-five years ago, Carole was a home economics teacher, and she was always making something.

"I'd come home from work, sit here, read a magazine, smoke a pipe while Carole worked, and I realized I, too, wanted to do something. So I tried making candles, but that was about the time of the oil embargo, and the price of wax skyrocketed. Then I tried macrame when that was the big rage, but that was te-dious work, tying all those knots."

But when Carole showed him some magazines containing wood items, Ed was intrigued. He explains, "Dad had a band saw and a radial arm saw and a couple of other tools. He had built a couple of houses, and I had helped out. I did all the finishing work for him. So I had some background in woodworking."

Ed started small, borrowing tools from his dad, working from plans in magazines. But even at the start, he was focused on generating extra income. "Making money was always a part of what we did. We weren't money hungry, but you have to be able to at least pay for your materials and your equipment. At that time, we had only been married for a few years, and we were thinking about having a family. We had expenses, so whatever we bought in the way of craft supplies, we had to pay for.

"We had a good friend, a teacher who worked with Carole, who was really into the craft scene. She was a potter, who later turned to weaving, and every year she did the big Winterfair show here in Columbus [a show held each year on the weekend after Thanksgiving]. I got to talking to her, and I said, 'What do you have to do to get in there?'

"She said, 'You really have to have your own designs.'

"Well, I was a frustrated engineer, and I did a lot of drafting in college. So I did some designs. I did a train, some trucks, some airplanes. In fact, still today, some of my best-selling items are ones I designed right there at the beginning.

"When our kids were growing up, I got ideas from some of the books they were reading—like the Richard Scarry books. Those books are wonderful sources of ideas. Also, we had been going to craft shows. We had seen what people were making. We had also seen what they weren't making, and at that time, there was nobody making realistic toy planes,

"Carole showed me some magazines. 'Here,' she said. 'Look at these wood items. Are you interested in these?'"

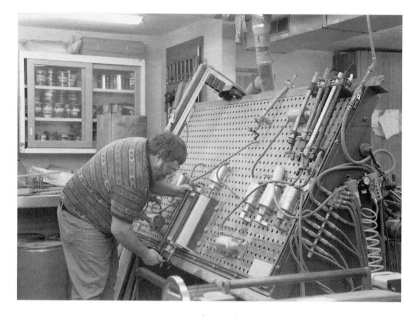

Ed is placing the body of a block wagon onto his clamping table.

"I still have to use pipe clamps, even when I'm using my clamping table," he explains.

Carole adds, "But you don't have to move them [pipe clamps] every time. It used to be that every time he came in the house, his legs would be all banged up because he was trying to get through some place where his legs didn't fit."

trucks and tractors.

"I had grown up on a farm. I had worked in construction, so when I sat down to design the toys, I just drew on what I knew."

Like many woodworkers, Ed learned his craft by doing it, making extensive use of trial and error. "I've never done any major pieces of furniture. But over the years, as I worked on my toys, I quickly learned what their failure points were: where a joint wasn't right, that kind of thing."

Growing the Business

In those first years, their product line was very modest. "We probably had 20 pieces when we started doing shows." But over the years, in response to customer requests, the line expanded. "People would come in, and they would say, 'Can you make a garbage truck?'

"And I would say, 'Yeah. Do you have any pictures?'

"One day Mrs. Anderson [of the Anderson family involved in the ready-mix concrete business in central Ohio] came in and said, 'Do you have a concrete mixer?'

"I had a little miniature one that I had made from a pattern. I said: 'Yeah, I have a little one up there on the shelf.'

"She said, 'No. I want something bigger, something 12 or 14 inches long.'

"At that time, I did some custom work—built toys to order—if I thought the toy had potential for becoming a line item. Occasionally, I would do a single copy, and if I found that it was too complicated, I would never make another.

"So I told Mrs. Anderson, 'Here's my card. Put your name and phone number on the back of it, and when I get a chance, I'll call you. I've been thinking about designing one anyway.'

"So she handed me the card and I saw her name on the back: Mrs. Ralph Anderson. I immediately realized who she was.

"The following spring we were doing the Arts Festival in downtown Columbus. It was when they were building the Hyatt and starting Capital Square, and the Andersons had a couple of their concrete trucks down there.

"So I said, 'That's what I need.' I was having some trouble getting the drum profile, so I went home early, grabbed the camera, took some pictures, then designed the truck. I made two or three of them, but I never got around to calling Mrs. Anderson.

"The following winter, a friend of ours was taking some publicity shots for local newspapers in connection with Winterfair. He came over to our shop and took a picture of us holding a concrete mixer. The picture appeared in the *Reynoldsburg Reporter*.

"On Wednesday we went to set up for Winterfair, and that night we got a call from the Executive Director of the Central Ohio Concrete Association. He'd seen the picture in the Reynoldsburg paper. He said, 'Did you make that?'

"I said, 'Yeah.'

"He said, 'Can I come over and get one?'

"So he got the first one. I also had one in the booth during the first two days of Winterfair, but it didn't sell.

"Then we were sitting around Saturday morning having brunch at Winterfair with the publicity director for the show. I told her the whole story, and she said, 'Molly Anderson is my next-door neighbor. Give me that concrete truck. I know she wants it.'

"So I wrapped it up and gave it to her. Then the next day, she came in and said, 'She was so pleased with that truck she was just beside herself.'

"Now, I'd put a bill in the bag, but I didn't hear from Mrs. Anderson. So a month or two later, I called her, and she said, 'Oh my gosh. I didn't want Ralph to find it, so I hid it in the attic and then I forgot about it.'

"So she got it out and gave it to him and sent me a check right away. And ever since then, the Andersons have called me periodically to order concrete trucks to give out as retirement gifts.

"I don't know how many times people came in and requested special toys, and that's how our collection has evolved."

Tooling the Shop

"For the basic bread-and-butter items, you have to be able to crank out a lot of work, and the only way you can do that is with good-quality equipment."

"When I started out, all I had was a little Craftsman band saw and a 6″ × 48″ belt sander. Then I went out and bought a drill press and a small Craftsman lathe."

It wasn't long, however, before Ed learned that his consumer-grade equipment, although perfectly satisfactory for occasional use, simply couldn't stand up to hours of slogging through hardwood.

"I was just tearing up the band saw trying to cut 8/4 stock. So I went out and got a table saw, a little Craftsman.

"I learned at the craft shows what people wanted in the way of toys and what they were willing to pay for those toys. So I decided pretty quickly that I had to rely on good power equipment.

"I went to the wood shows. I saw the equipment; I saw what it could do. In fact, years ago, they would even let you run the equipment at the shows. I also talked to friends who did different kinds of woodworking, and I learned from them.

"One friend, who was a pipe maker, had a spindle sander just like the one I use now. At that time, I was using a drum on a drill press, running the spindle up and down to smooth curved edges. I saw this spindle sander and realized right away that that machine could save me a ton of time."

The high-tech, high-quality equipment has allowed Ed to keep his prices low while still providing his customers with the quality they demand. "I felt driven to go high-tech with my tools because, in order to do quality work and maintain enough inventory to do quality shows, I had to produce a lot of work in

"For the basic bread-and-butter items, you have to be able to crank out a lot of work, and the only way you can do that is with good-quality equipment."

On the left, the body of a high-sided wagon is clamped. On the right, the body of a low-sided wagon is clamped.

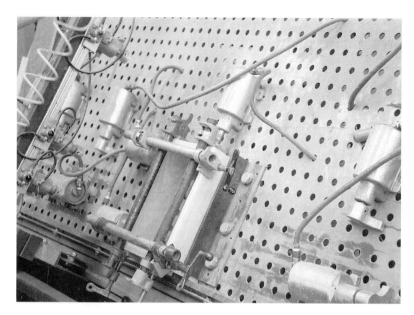

This detail shows the compressed-air-driven cylinders that do the actual clamping. They can be lifted and repositioned into new locations on the table's surface in seconds.

"Two years ago, we did eight shows, and that was too much."

a hurry. I'm also not inclined, by nature, to do a lot of handwork."

Ed, in his continual search for better and faster ways to produce his toys, has never stopped adding to his stock of power equipment. "I make a bunch of block wagons every year, and when you start ripping stock for the blocks, you need some solid equipment. My original table saw just gave out. The motor kept shutting down, and the fence wasn't true anymore. So then I got a big 5 hp Powermatic Model 66. And during the last two years, I've been seriously considering a power feeder for my table saw. What I'm trying to do now is buy tools and attachments that will make life in the shop easier."

Although he tries to keep up with the maintenance of his shop equipment, he's not obsessive about that particular aspect of woodworking. "I don't enjoy tool maintenance and setup. It's a necessary evil. Just yesterday, I was changing planer blades, and I realized I had my spare set wrapped in newspaper dated July 1994. I thought, 'Has it really been two and a half years since I changed the blades?'"

Ed laughs. "Then I looked at the blades, and I said, 'Yeah. It's been two and a half years.'"

One of the most important additions to Ed's shop is an enormous, infinitely adjustable gluing table, complete with compressed-air-driven clamps. "My gluing press saves a terrific amount of time and effort. Before I had that, I was using a squaring jig built of plywood and angle iron. It was very heavy, and I was constantly picking it up and moving it around—and I have a bad back, anyhow. So I went shopping. I started looking for some kind of gluing press. I looked at about five different models before I found the one I bought."

The longer he practices his craft, the more certain Ed becomes that high-quality power equipment is an indispensable part of his operation. "We're working in what is probably the most machine-intensive craft on the show circuit. More than glass blowers and jewelers, potters and weavers. More even than some other kinds of woodworkers. A Windsor chair built by hand might sell for $800 apiece. That's equal to the price of 16 of my trains. So I've got to build 16 pieces for every 1 that chair-maker builds. If you're making toys, you have to find ways to increase your speed. That's the only way to keep your prices competitive."

Selling the Toys

"Two years ago, we did eight shows, and that was too much."

"When we first started, we did a couple of little shows. Then we did Octoberfest, which at that time, was at the Ohio State Fairgrounds. Then we started doing Winterfair, which we've done now for 18 years.

"Now we also do Columbus Arts Festival and the State College Festival in Pennsylvania. We also do two shows in Michigan: Birmingham, and Arts and Apples. Arts and Apples is probably the sixth- or seventh-rated show in the country."

Although Ed is nearing retirement, he still has a full-time job as a process engineer. Ed and Carole are able to do so many shows each year only because Ed has earned many vacation days during his tenure with his company.

"One year we did several East Coast shows, although we didn't do very well. I just wanted to see who was out there. You see all the literature for these shows, and in the photos, there are all these very elaborate toys. What we found is that while some of these guys have three or four showpieces, the rest of their toys—the ones they're actually selling—are just cut out of 2×4s.

"Now, you would think that the promoters would catch on after awhile, but many are just interested in the booth fee and the gate fee. They claim that they care about the artists, but I don't know if that's always true."

Ed and Carole, like many other artists on the craft-show circuit, have found that while some promoters seem uninterested in the success of the artists, others are very helpful. "Some promoters simply manage their shows better than others. I think the best are those that are run by arts organizations. Arts and Apples is run by the Paint Creek Art Association. All volunteers, and they know how to put on a show. That is one organization that knows how to take care of its artists. They meet you at the gate. They direct you to your booth. They solve any problems you have getting set up. They come around bringing doughnuts and coffee in the morning. They're just good people.

"At other shows, the promoters are just out there to make a buck. The booth fees may be double what they should be. They may have a private showing the Friday night before the show, which the artists have to attend, and all the promot-

ers are doing is wining and dining their clients. And the artist may only sell a hundred bucks that night or nothing at all."

The Schmidts have also noted a diminishment in the quality of some shows that might have been quite good just ten years earlier. "Many are not as successful today as they were in years past. I know at several our sales volume is down. Some of these shows are losing their top-name artists because sales have slipped so badly. Partly that's because there are too many exhibitors. A show that once might have had 200 booths now has 375. That means each booth is going to make less."

To supplement their sales at retail shows, Ed and Carole have produced a 12-page, fully illustrated catalog. Carole explains their approach to the catalog: "We do one every three or four years. Then we do a separate price list. That way we can change prices without reprinting the catalog. We give out copies with every purchase, and we get a lot of repeat sales that way. In fact we've shipped a lot of orders this year, way more than we have in the past."

Although catalog sales provide them with a steady, year-round income, the process is not without its problems. In

This mortising machine has allowed Ed to bore axle mortises that are both 90° from the stock's jointed edge and parallel to the stock's lower surface.

"I saw this at a wood show in Atlanta. Before, when I'd drill axle holes, the bit might wander a little, so I'd end up with only three of four wheels on the ground. Now I drill on either side and put a short axle with just one wheel on it on each end. This gives me an accurate 90° angle, so all four wheels sit on the ground at the same time."

addition to the obvious complexities of packing and shipping, there is also the burden of maintaining an inventory of the dozens of different toys they sell. "I hate it when I get a catalog order for something that isn't in stock," Ed explains. "That means I have to go out and set up to make a run of that particular item just to get that one piece.

"Generally, I try to keep trains, airplanes, block wagons, farm tractors, bulldozer sets—the basics—in stock all the time. The big semis—I have eight different styles—I try to keep them in stock also. At the end of the year, I'll usually have 200 pieces in inventory."

Ed and Carole both admit they couldn't sustain their business through catalog sales alone. They see the high-quality retail shows, however frustrating they might sometimes be, as an essential part of their business. Also, as Carole points out, "We enjoy the contact with the public. It's fun to see the kids play with the toys. It's fun to hear the customers' comments about the toys."

In this connection, Ed mentions the pleasures of repeat business. "People come back year after year. We've been doing this for almost 25 years, doing the major shows for more than 15 years. And people will come back and say, 'I've got this, this and this. What's new?'

"Others will say, 'I got a couple of these pieces for my kids. Now I'm buying for my grandkids.'

"Others will say, 'That train has been through three of our kids, five of the neighbor kids. Now it's going to the grandkids.'

To maintain this good rapport with their customers, the Schmidts repair or replace, without cost, any toy that's broken. "We sand them down, put on some new finish, and they're as good as new. All we ask is reimbursement for shipping costs.

"We have a good friend who's now a V.P. at The Limited. She bought an aerial truck for her son, and he played with it all the time. He was very careful with it, but one day he took it to school for show-and-tell. The kids really got rough with it and knocked the top of the cab off. His mom was pretty upset. She called and I said, 'Don't worry about it. Just bring it in.' And she did, and we fixed it up, and you couldn't tell it had been broken."

Ed admits to being frustrated in his attempts to wholesale. "We've tried wholesaling several times, but most people want half of your retail price, and we can't sell our toys for that little. And they won't sell for double my price, although there are some places that have tried it. Normally, I'll discount my stuff about 25 percent when I'm wholesaling. I can do that because I figure about 25 percent of the price of each toy is show fees, travel, etc."

Planning Production Runs

The number of pieces Ed produces in an individual production run is dependent upon a number of variables. Perhaps the most important of these is the number of copies of a particular toy that he expects to sell during the coming year. "I know, for example, that I'm going to sell close to a hundred trains every year. I know that I'm going to sell at least a hundred each of two or three different airplanes."

At this point, Carole interrupts with a wry smile. "It also depends on how many you can stand to make at one time." Carole cautions against the dangers of an excessively large production run: "We did 60 trains at one time, and we can't stand to make 60 trains."

Ed laughs, indicating his wife with a nod of his head. "I could make them, but Carole couldn't. She does all the finishing."

Carole agrees with Ed's assessment. "I get bored with that many."

Ed estimates that he rarely does more than 30 of any particular type in one run. "One thing I've noticed is that if I do a whole lot of any one thing, I have arm fatigue, and I end up with carpal tunnel syndrome. In fact I've had surgery on both hands. Since then I've learned that change is good.

"For the most part, I work in runs of 25 to 30 pieces. But when I'm making the bigger trucks—the dump trucks, the aerial trucks, things like that—I'll only make six or eight. That's because at any one show I'm not going to sell five or ten of these big trucks. I may only sell one or two or three. So if I make six or eight, I've got enough for two or three shows."

Although each piece in a production run of 30 trains is identical, Ed and Carole do permit their customers to mix and match parts from several trains before buying. "Even though all the trains in a run are made from the same material, there can be different grain patterns. In the case of the trains, that means maple for the bases, birch dowel stock for the boilers and the tankers, elm or walnut for the rest."

Ed has found that it's better to buy certain parts from suppliers than it is to make them himself. "I don't make any wheels; those I buy. The wheels that I use on the trains and airplanes are only four cents apiece, but I buy in lots of 20,000."

Although he doesn't make the wheels, he admits that he might have several hours' time invested in assembling the undercarriages of the vehicles in a particular production run.

Once the complicated axle assemblies are completed, they are finished before the axles are mounted on the vehicle bodies. "We put polyurethane varnish on

This is a close-up of the laser etching that Ed uses to ornament the surface of certain toys. The work is done by a local sign shop.

the wheels because it's a harder finish. Then we put Deft on everything else. On big trucks, we put two coats of finish; on everything else, generally three coats, sanding between each coat."

Carole does all the sanding by hand, using 320-grit wet/dry paper between each coat. One advantage of the smaller production run is a reduced period of hand sanding, a process that has occasionally taken a toll on Carole's hands. Ed explains, "When I was running behind on inventory and we were making 60 pieces at a time, the constant sanding would wear the skin off Carole's fingers."

Carole, who does the finishing in the house, works in the basement during the winter and circulates the air with fans. In the spring, summer and fall, she works on a screened-in porch. "I've got the fun part," she explains. "I get to put on the finish, and that's when the grain comes out."

Ed, too, is always anxious to see the toys after the application of that first coat of finish. "I try to match up colors in the shop, but I like to come in the house after she's got that first coat on just to see what it really looks like."

As much as possible, Ed uses figured

and contrasting woods for his toys. "The price of materials only accounts for about 10 percent of the cost of the finished toy. And I can't make enough stuff out of bird's-eye.

"I've also made a lot of stuff from Western quilted maple. It's terrible to work with. It has little tufts in the quilted areas, and it's terrible to sand out. When I run it through the drum sander and run it slow, it burns. The only way I can sand it is to take very light cuts and run my table just as fast as it will go. But it is a beautiful wood."

Ed has done time studies of the construction of several of his pieces. To calculate prices, he estimates a labor cost of $20 per hour. Recently, he also did an overhead study—examining insurance costs, travel and show costs, utilities, bank fees—that indicated an additional $6 per hour needed to be added to his shop time. But Ed admits that even this overhead figure doesn't include compensation for shop cleanup time and tool maintenance time.

Doing What They Love

We all make decisions about how we're going to spend our time. Ed and Carole Schmidt, who together operate Toys 'n' Stuff, have made decisions about how to spend their time, and each has chosen to focus on those parts of the toy-making trade they most enjoy. For Ed, the best part of the process may be the implementation of production runs in his well-equipped shop. For Carole, the best part may be the application of the finish, a process that reveals the beauty of the materials Ed works with.

Both also enjoy the contact with the buying public that attend various retail shows they do each year. There, they get to witness firsthand the pleasure their carefully crafted toys bring to the children who will play with them and to the adults who are reminded of the sturdy toys they themselves once enjoyed.

This bulldozer and soil compactor reflect Ed's interest in heavy machinery.

This multiaxle dump truck, done in contrasting woods, has been a customer favorite.

This aerial truck comes complete with figures in the cab and a figure in the bucket.

The articulated midsection of this roller makes this toy a bit more difficult to build but also makes it a bit more appealing to own.

Laser-etched lettering has become a key design element in several of the Schmidts' toys.

JODY GRAY CHAPMAN

The Elegant Conception of Jigs and Fixtures

This mantle clock is modeled after a pillow block bearing.

FOCUS: With the aid of dozens of elegantly conceived jigs and fixtures, Jody Gray Chapman and her partner, James Wilson Lindsey, produce hundreds of clocks and household accessories in their shop outside Newark, Ohio. Their operation is based on several principles: (1) Jigs and fixtures—some of their own design, many the work of Jody's uncle J.R. Beall—make it possible to produce dozens (or even hundreds) of copies of a part while maintaining consistently high standards of quality; (2) A well-organized shop permits efficient production work; and (3) High-quality machinery kept in superb condition is an essential part of the production process.

I t is the last day of an uncommonly warm January in central Ohio. Although—intimidated by the calendar—I wear a coat, the air is warm and springlike, the sky a cloudless blue.

As I load my arms with camera, tripod and tape recorder from the trunk of my car, a woman appears at the door of the large, metal-sided building at the rear of the gravel parking area.

I step forward, offering a hand. "Jody?"

She is young, not yet 30, wearing blue jeans and a sweater patterned in several shades of pink and white. Her long, blond hair is pulled back in a ponytail. She smiles warmly and shakes my hand. "Pleased to meet you. Do you need any help with those things?"

I don't find the woodworking field to be particularly sexist, but it is a fact that of the 23 woodworkers I've profiled for books and magazines, only four have been women. Two of those four didn't actually work the wood; they concentrated instead on applying paint and finishes while their husbands did the cutting and fitting and shaping.

That Jody is a female craftsperson who actually works the wood makes her rare. That she is both female and young (well shy of middle age) makes her, at least in my experience, unique.

We enter the metal-sided building into an office space. A desk stands to the right, with storage cabinets dead ahead and to the left. She guides me to the left, through a doorway, into another office. Wooden clocks are hung on the walls and stand on a rack of shelves. Other wooden items—a rocking blotter, a magnifying glass with a wooden bezel and a turned wooden handle, as well as a small wooden chest which I later learn is to be converted into a humidor—are scattered around the room. Although cluttered, the room

Dowel stock is stored in this rack.

is clean, bright, airy.

Jody directs me to place my things on a large, round table in the center of the room. We sit and begin to talk.

A few moments later a man enters the room. This I learn is J.R. Beall, the founder of the company and Jody's uncle. His hair is gray. He wears suspenders over a casual shirt.

"I never did anything for a hobby. I went into it to make a buck."

J.R. Beall's woodworking experience goes back almost 30 years. He explains, "I started building musical instruments in 1969. Actually, I guess it was 1969 when I went into woodworking full-time. It didn't take very long before I realized that I would rather do woodwork than work at AT&T."

In 1978, he started the line of clocks which would become, over the next two decades, the heart and soul of his business. By combining shrewdly designed fixtures with hand-shaped detail, he was able to offer the public a variety of clocks housed in attractive hardwood cases at very reasonable prices.

In the early 1980s, he began making and selling devices for cutting threads in

"I never did anything for a hobby. I went into it to make a buck."

J.R. Beall

This cardboard box has been partitioned in order to separate various grits of sandpaper.

"I grew up just up the hill from here, and I was always down here, knocking around."

wood. To publicize these devices, he used his self-published book, *The Nuts and Bolts of Woodworking*. "We knew we didn't really need that many people to be involved in the publishing process. If we did all that work—the writing, the photography and everything—we wanted more than 8 percent royalties, and we made all our money back in the first two months. We printed 15,000, and although we have a lot left, it's wonderful to have them. We can offer them as bonuses and giveaways with our tools."

In addition to J.R.'s threading devices, the company offers a number of other woodworking tools, some of which are available through the Harteville and Leigh Valley catalogs.

J.R. explains his approach to woodworking. "What I am is a mechanic. If you're going to be a woodworker, you've got to be a mechanic." This trait, he believes, has permitted him to design and build dozens of jigs and fixtures that make possible the rapid and accurate manufacture of wooden parts.

Although he admits that the repetitiveness of the production-run process can be wearying, he remains strongly committed to this approach. "It speeds things up when you can do a volume of an item. When we were making magnify-

ing glasses, we made thousands and thousands of them." And according to J.R., this level of productivity couldn't have been achieved without the efficiencies of the production-run process.

This commitment to the production run is shared by his niece, Jody Gray Chapman. With her partner, James Wilson Lindsey (Jay), Jody bought the woodworking portion of J. + J. Beall from her uncle in March 1996.

"I grew up just up the hill from here, and I was always down here, knocking around."

Jody's earliest memories of working are centered on the company she now owns. "I have a brother and two sisters. When we were kids, we'd come down and sweep the shop and box stuff up, whatever we could do. Then, after my first year of college, I got a summer job here."

That summer she realized she preferred working in her uncle's shop to working in a college classroom. "I liked woodworking, and I didn't want to go back to college. I didn't feel like I had any direction. I didn't know what my major was going to be. College just seemed pointless.

"I was going to Miami [University] of Ohio. It's a good school, but it's oriented toward business, and I wasn't even sure that was what I wanted to do. And although I'm in business now, it's a different kind than I was thinking of then.

"So I said to J.R., 'Can I have a full-time job instead of just a summer job?' And he needed me—there were never enough people—so J.R. said, 'Sure.'

"There were two guys with me for three or four years. Then they became more career oriented and went on to other jobs. Then it was just me, and I was doing all the production stuff. J.R. and his wife, Judith, were doing the business end of it."

Then, after more than 20 years of production woodworking, J.R. decided he needed a change. Jody explains, "He wanted to get out of it. He'd been saying for years that he wanted to do other things. He was sick of the clocks. He wanted to invent some new stuff.

"So he asked me if I'd be interested in buying the business, and I said, 'Sure.' And that was it. It took a while to materialize, but it did happen."

To help shoulder the responsibilities of her new business, Jody took on a partner. "My partner is my boyfriend. He was working with concrete, and he wasn't happy in that business. It's a strenuous job, and he has back problems and foot problems. The money was good in the summer, but there was always a slow period in the winter. And he's a really good woodworker. So I asked him, and he agreed. So we've been doing it together for a year."

Growing the Business

"This year we're doing a lot of retail shows. We're trying to do more of those this year because our regular business doesn't pick up until we get closer to Christmas."

When Jody and her partner purchased J.R. Beall's woodworking business in 1996, they received, as part of that purchase, a number of wholesale customers. Jody explains, "J.R. had already established a pretty wide network of customers, and we still do business with them." In addition, Jody and her partner advertise to attract new wholesale customers. "We do ads in the *Crafts Report*. People see our ads and contact us and ask us to send them a catalog. Then they place an order."

Sometimes wholesale clients come to them requiring custom work. "We had a couple of exclusive contracts with Levenger's. They didn't want anybody else [other wholesalers] buying these items. We made thousands of reproduction antique magnifying glasses for them. We've also made them a number of music stands."

While wholesale customers account for the biggest share of current sales, Jody and her partner are aggressively pursuing retail customers. "Right now our retail sales account for less than 25

> "This year we're doing a lot of retail shows. We're trying to do more of those this year because our regular business doesn't pick up until we get closer to Christmas."

Rolling tables are used to move parts from one operation to the next.

percent of our income. We would like to see that change."

To attract these customers, they have begun doing retail shows, the most important of which is Winterfair in Columbus, Ohio. "Winterfair was really good this year. J.R. used to do it, but this is our first year as Wilson Gray."

Jody explains that it's difficult to predict how many copies of a particular item might be sold at a particular show. "We never know what we're going to sell, so it's hard to know what to take. We always run out of something, and we always have some item that nobody buys. Although we do know that the small-ticket items are going to sell the best, so we take more of those. We take maybe 30 or 40 different big clocks, then maybe 30 of the small ones.

"We also make some stuff just for shows. Right now I'm working on a bunch of cutting boards we're making from our scrap. We can sell these at a show because they don't have to be something that we make in production and sell out of our catalog."

Jody sees a diverse product line as one of the keys to their future success. "Right now there are probably 50 items in our line if you count the music stand, the magnifying glass and the rocking blotter. We've made a lot of unusual items that aren't necessarily clocks." The number of nonclock items has grown in the last year, as Jody and her partner have added new products to their line.

In order to encompass this growing diversity of product, Jody and her partner have changed the name of the business from J.+J. Beall Clocks to Wilson Gray Woodworks.

"We want to expand out of clocks. Our goal is to expand, to eventually have a whole line of small household accessories: candlesticks, towel racks, small decorative items."

> "Usually we decide what we're going to make, then how we're going to make it. You know, we could do it this way or we could do it that way—what's going to be easier?"

Engineering the Product

"Usually we decide what we're going to make, then how we're going to make it. You know, we could do it this way or we could do it that way— what's going to be easier?"

Every new product begins with an idea. Some ideas are generated by Jody and her partner; others come from outside sources. "Sometimes we get ideas from magazines. Sometimes we get ideas from customers. For instance, we had a meeting with ODC [Ohio Designer Craftsmen], and they told us what they thought would sell.

"Usually, we next make a couple of copies the hard way (one-of-a-kind-construction). We may then modify the idea to make it simpler to make. Then we build jigs and fixtures that will allow us to make a whole lot of them.

"We sort of engineer in reverse. We see what we want as a whole, then we break it into parts. Then we ask ourselves, 'What would be the easiest way to make this part?'

"J.R. still helps with the design. He'll sit down, and he'll say, 'Well, you could do it like this or this or this.' Then I'll have something to look at. Then I can decide what I want to do."

Cost-effective design is a critical issue in the engineering process. "We ask ourselves, 'Can we make this piece at a reasonable cost, or should we change the design?'"

Then finally, after much planning and many redesigns, the product is ready for its first production run. "When we've got 10 or 20 copies made using the fixtures, we get photographs and let people know what we have."

The Elegant Conception of Jigs and Fixtures

Accustomed to the cluttered and chaotic environs of my own shop, I find Jody's shop to be a revelation. It is clean, well lighted, organized. At each of the dozens of workstations, tools and materials are neatly arranged to permit speedy and efficient work. Shavings aren't permitted to pile up in waist-deep drifts. Tools are carefully maintained. And everywhere I look I see cleverly conceived and meticulously executed jigs and fixtures.

But this is not idiot-proof woodworking. Even though the jigs and fixtures—as well as some of the automated machinery—make it possible to routinely manufacture thousands of wooden items while maintaining a high level of quality, it is obvious that Jody has a thorough understanding of the woodworking discipline.

When she stands at the short-bed lathe turning the bead on a clock bezel with a handheld tool, shavings are directed expertly from the cutting edge. When she speaks about the material with which she works, she talks about designing to accommodate expansion and contraction. When she puts a fixture into place, her hands are deft and sure.

Jody Gray Chapman understands her craft.

This stately desk clock is named the "Parliament," a reference to a time when the English Parliament taxed all clocks.

This clock is known by several names, one of which is "Napoleon's Hat." Standing on four brass bun feet, this particular model is crafted of bubinga.

This mantle clock, the "Grecian," is patterned after one dating back to 1870.

This clock features a functioning nut and bolt.

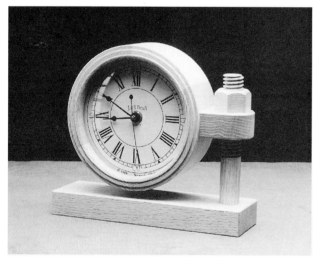

The face of this screw-post clock hovers above the base, held there by the post.

This desk clock, the "Arch Top," is identified by a band of inlay reaching from the face to the base.

Threading Machine

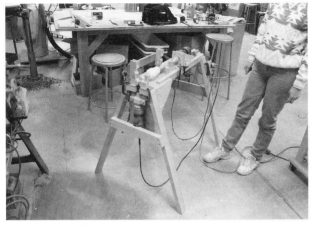

PHOTO 1. Threads can be cut in wood very quickly using this shop-made device.

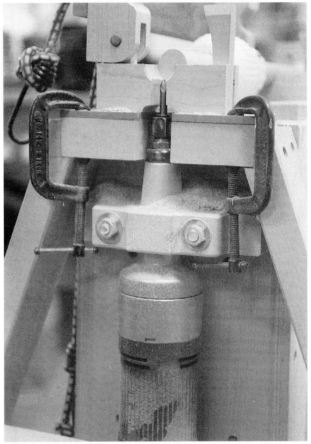

PHOTO 2. The thread-cutting bit is powered by a die grinder. Here a length of dowel stock can be seen lying in position ready to be clamped in place.

PHOTO 3. The dowel stock has been clamped in place and fed past the thread-cutting bit. Notice the bungee cord that holds the clamping blocks against the dowel stock. Notice, too, the length of threaded dowel behind the nylon chuck into which the unthreaded dowel is fit. That length of threaded dowel passes through a threaded block, feeding the unthreaded dowel past the bit at the proper rate.

Making Clock Bodies

PHOTO 1. "For these clocks we start out with six blocks. Then we sand the angle to a precise 30° on the disc sander. This gives you a smooth, tight joint."

PHOTO 2. "We use a band clamp to glue them up. Right now we use regular Tite Bond. Then after it's glued up, we use this little spring-loaded fixture to mark it so we know where to drill our holes. This fixture is something J.R. designed 20 years ago."

PHOTO 3. Then, with a cordless drill, Jody attaches a faceplate to the hexagon. "This cordless drill is one of the most useful tools in the shop."

PHOTO 4. The faceplate is turned onto the lathe's threaded headstock.

PHOTO 5. The automatic lathe then begins shaping the clock body.

PHOTO 6. The interior of the clock body is given its final shape on another automatic lathe. While that interior is being shaped, Jody sands the outside of the clock case.

PHOTO 7. The final shaping of the body is done on a short-bed lathe. Here Jody is shown turning the bead that will frame the clock face. These are all turned by hand, and each bead is different, which makes each clock a one-of-a-kind item.

PHOTO 8 + 9. Final sanding of the clock's exterior is done on this machine. Notice that the clock body is held in place by the expansion of the three interior jaws.

PHOTO 10. Clock backs are cut on this circle-cutting jig mounted to a band saw. Notice the tiny pin sticking up in the jig's dead center.

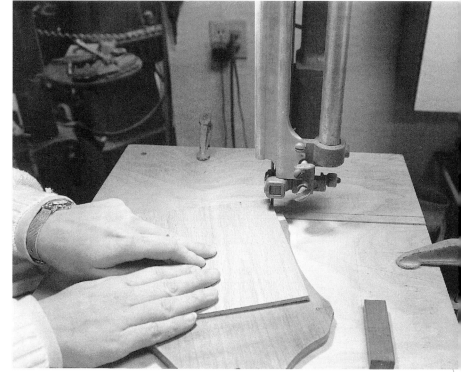

PHOTO 11. Here a square of plywood has been mounted on the jig with its center located by the pin.

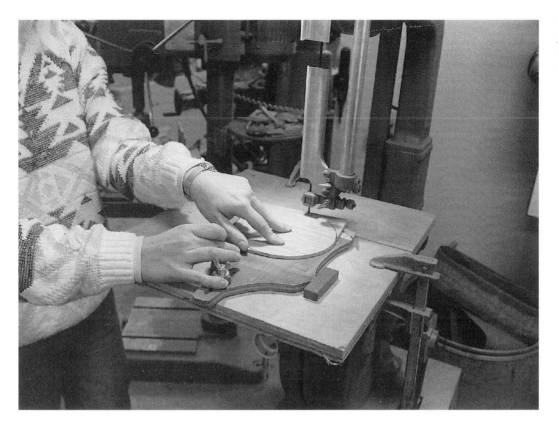

PHOTO 12.
Jody completes the cutting of a clock back.

PHOTO 13. The final sizing is done on a router table with the plywood disc being held in place through the use of a vacuum clamp. To activate the clamp, Jody places the disc up against the foam on the bottom of the clamp. She then moves her thumb so that it covers the small hole visible on the clamp's handle. The vacuum is then activated.

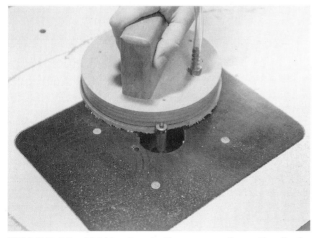

PHOTO 14. Held in place by the vacuum clamp, the disc is passed around a flush trim bit.

PHOTO 15. The raw edge is then smoothed on a stationary belt sander.

Making Wooden Nuts

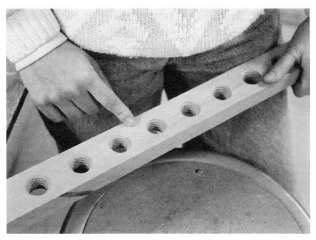

PHOTO 1. Holes are drilled through a length of stock, then tapped on a drill press.

PHOTO 2. Using this sliding carriage, individual nuts are separated from the stock.

PHOTO 3. The peg shown here allows the operator to feed the stock across the saw blade at the right point.

PHOTO 4. The nuts are held in plastic tubs awaiting the next step in the process.

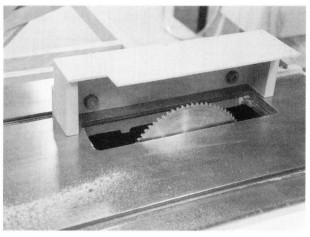

PHOTO 5. This apparatus is used to gang cut the hexagonal sides of the nuts.

PHOTO 6. Prior to the cutting of the hexagonal sides, the nuts are stacked on this dowel. A smaller nut is then tightened onto the threaded end, holding the nuts securely in place.

PHOTO 7. Seen from the fence side of the blade, this is the custom-made guard for the gang-cutting apparatus.

PHOTO 8. Seen from the opposite side of the blade, this is the fixture that carries the nut stock past the blade. Notice that the dowel on which the nuts were fit earlier is aligned parallel to the blade. Notice also the six grooves milled into the dowel's left end. These grooves fit onto a key set into the fixture's body.

PHOTO 9. This photo shows that key.

PHOTO 10. These stickers indicate fence settings for the various nuts Jody manufactures.

PHOTO 11. After the hexagonal sides have been cut, Jody gang sands the nuts before removing them from the dowel.

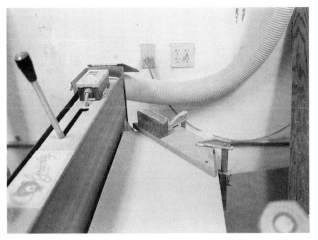

PHOTO 12. This jig positions individual nuts in a way that permits the belt sander to produce the crowned bevels on the top sides of each nut.

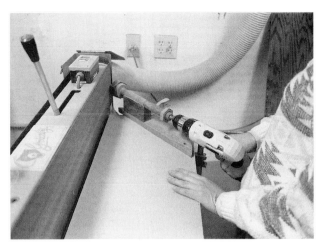

PHOTO 13. A cordless drill spins each nut against the sanding belt.

PHOTO 14. After sanding, each nut is given a single coat of Minwax. The nuts shown here are drying on a shelf in Jody's finishing room.

PHOTO 15. The nuts are polished on a charged wheel.

CHAPTER SEVEN

The Use of the Workstation

The addition of props turns some of his dancers into narrative sculpture.

FOCUS: In his hillside operation near Caldwell, Ohio, Bill Saling makes several thousand clog dancers each year, combining production-run techniques with hand-executed, one-of-a-kind detailing. In an effort to keep himself mentally fresh while maintaining this high level of productivity, Bill breaks his workday into a number of different segments, each spent at one of the many workstations he's located in his shop, in his studio and in his house.

Bill Saling lives and works on a hillside in southeastern Ohio. His shop and his studio are perched high above his house on a slope so steep that climbing it turns my legs into Jell-O.

I pause halfway up, resting on steps built of 4×4s pegged into the ground with lengths of reinforcing rod. I admire the view through a stand of trees winter has stripped of leaves. Below me, I see the roof of his white frame house. Beyond the house, on the other side of the narrow highway, pasture rolls off into the distance.

"Great view," I say, trying to conceal my breathlessness. "Great place for a shop."

He nods his agreement, then leads me on. I bend to the task of climbing. Above us on our left, a building the size of a small house rises on a foundation of concrete blocks. Turning, speaking to me over his shoulder, he explains this is his studio, where he assembles his dancers.

We climb on. Finally, on our right, reaching out over the slope, its floor supported on wooden stilts on the downhill side, Bill's shop comes into view.

When we arrive at the door, Bill pushes it open, allowing me to enter first. The shop is warm, heated by a small-bodied wood burner. Bill removes his coat and checks the fire. I look around.

Although the shop contains a fairly complete selection of power tools—table saw, band saw, scroll saw, flexible disc sander and flap sander—all are of the home-owner variety. Several benches, scattered with a selection of hand tools and bits of shaped wood, are situated in various locations. Racks hang on the front wall and above a central bench, and within the compartments of those racks, I see what I later learn are arms, legs and torsos for dancers currently under construction.

What I don't see is material storage. I turn, looking for the racks of hardwood tucked away in every woodworker's shop, but there are none. There is, in fact, no hardwood visible anywhere. "Where do you keep your material?" I ask.

"Right here," he explains, his hand tapping a stack of 2×4s laid across his table saw.

"You use 2×4s?" I keep my voice neutral, anxious not to judge.

Bill nods.

I cock my head to one side and make a vague gesture with my hands. "But what were the dancers made of historically?"

"Whatever was there. Sure, a lot of them were made out of hardwood, but others were made out of scrap. Bits of soft wood. Whatever was there. They also went through a period when they were made out of discarded wooden shipping crates."

I reflect on this. "I guess I expected to see hardwood."

Bill nods and smiles.

Getting Into Woodworking

"I don't know that I could go back to teaching now. I just enjoy my independence so much, although I put in more hours than ever. A 14-hour day is fairly standard."

After graduating from Ohio State University, Bill Saling served in the army for two and a half years, working in military intelligence. He spent a year of that enlistment in Turkey, then a year and a half here in the U.S. After leaving the service, he took a job as a high school art teacher in Caldwell, Ohio, and worked in that capacity for 18 years.

"I enjoyed teaching high school art. The only reason I'm out of it now is that

"I don't know that I could go back to teaching now. I just enjoy my independence so much, although I put in more hours than ever. A 14-hour day is fairly standard."

Bill pauses to talk en route from his shop to his studio.

I just burned out. It was because I was trying to keep up with this here." With a wave of his hand, he indicates the materials and dancers in his painting studio. "I didn't do the volume that I do now. But the thing is I just wanted to explore some other possibilities for a year.

"In fact I wanted to eventually return to teaching, but the board of education wouldn't give me a leave of absence. When they turned me down, my Dutch stubbornness came out, and I said, 'Sorry. I don't need teaching to make a living. I'm going to do what I want to do for awhile.'"

Indirectly, his college-level art experiences led him into the business of making clog dancers. "My training as an art teacher was poor. I don't think any of the professors that taught me had been in the classroom since God was a boy. The biggest problem was that the painting that I was expected to produce in college was painting that had been popular in New York in the 1920s, and this was 1967, 1968, 1969."

Bill sighs and adjusts his pipe. "After graduation, I took some of these big, colorful abstract paintings to shows and had

no luck selling them." He was then discovering what many others have discovered before and since: There is little demand for the kind of academic painting often taught in the nation's art schools. Realizing this, he began to look for another outlet for his creative aspirations.

"I had seen one of these dancers at a show in Michigan. I didn't even get to see it work. This lady and her husband were selling dulcimers. The man started playing his dulcimer, and she sat down on his case, on a paddle, with a dancer on a stick. But just then her child threw a fit, so I never did get to see the dancer being played.

"Anyway I brought the idea home with me because I thought this had to be something. And I made one, but by the time I'd finished a real short tune, the dancer had disintegrated."

At that time, Bill was working solely from his memory of that one dancer he'd seen in Michigan. He had no photos and no drawings for reference. But he was persistent, and eventually he began producing dancers that could take the punishment of being vigorously played, without the disintegration that had destroyed his first model.

"I had one or two of the dancers that I began to take to shows. I would sit on the curb and play with one to get people to stop and look at the paintings. But eventually, I had to be honest with myself. The paintings weren't selling. People would stop and say that they really liked my paintings, but then they would ask me how much I wanted for the dancer.

"After about the third show where that happened, I decided there wasn't any reason I couldn't express myself in a way that wouldn't also be financially viable. And that's what got me started selling the dancers.

"That first year, I produced 12. Last year, I produced 2800.

"It wasn't long before I stopped taking paintings to the shows. There are so many painters out there, really excellent painters, who are selling their work. With these dolls, there is not all that competition. I have a niche that's all mine."

Building the Product Line

"There are a lot of guys out there making the traditional, unpainted dancers. Some of them are also making other kinds of toys."

Dolls or musical instruments?

Bill explains that there is some disagreement about the function of the earliest clog dancers. "Some people considered them to be musical instruments, as part of the rhythm section. You know, on the back porch, with the fiddles and the banjos, they didn't have a trap set. So a lot of real simple ones were kept around for just that reason."

According to Bill, the original clog dancers were often quite plain. "They looked like jointed gingerbread people. Rarely were they painted, the attitude being that you wouldn't waste paint on a toy. They had one-piece arms. They had no feet. The leg just ended on the paddle."

It was this simple conception Bill began with 18 years ago. But it wasn't long before he was adding color, sculpture and whimsy to this classical mountain form. Now, as he explains, "My dancers are the only ones with this particular style."

His experimentation has changed not only the look of the dancers, it has also changed the sound the dancer makes on the paddle. "I've designed the feet so that you get a syncopated rhythm, more than just a single ticking sound. You get heel, toe, flat foot. You don't control it, but it's there, and it sounds like you control it."

Over the years, he has created dozens of different clog-dancing forms. "Right now, I have roughly 45 different characters. Some of these were suggested by customers. For example, one day someone came up to me and said, 'Do you do turtles? I collect turtles.' And I thought, 'Well, there isn't any reason why I couldn't try it.' So I did, and it felt good. But there are other characters a customer will suggest, and I'll just do one. It has to feel right to me.

"And there are some that I do very, very few of. I do a kangaroo with a joey in the pouch. Let's face it: That just takes an awful long time to make, and you really can't ask people to spend that much more.

"Just yesterday, I sent out a pair of dancers to a storyteller in Wisconsin. She wanted a Santa Claus, which I always have on hand, and she wanted a skeleton. Now a skeleton always takes a lot longer to do, and I won't always have one on hand, so I made a pair of them and sent her the best one of the two."

Recently, he had a customer who needed a dancer for a client who had an interest in tools, so Bill made one resembling Tim "The Tool Man" Taylor from *Home Improvement*. That same customer had a secretary who was into aviation, so Bill made a bird-shaped dancer

"There are a lot of guys out there making the traditional, unpainted dancers. Some of them are also making other kinds of toys."

In the painting workstation located in his house, Bill stands in front of a wall of finished dancers.

To make a dancer dance, Bill rhythmically taps his fist against the flexible wooden paddle on which the dancer's feet rest.

"Anything that you can do during a show to make noise will help. I know blacksmiths who just pound on their anvil. They're not making anything, but the noise makes folks stop and look."

wearing a flight jacket and goggles. This same customer also wanted a Grim Reaper dancer to give to an insurance adjuster. "That's not something I would ordinarily do, but they were fun to make. Jobs like that keep your juices flowing because, let's face it, there are some parts of this work that just aren't much fun."

Bill has also made special dancers for members of his family. "I have a niece who is attending Ohio University right now. So I fixed her up with an O.U. Bobcat. It had a green shirt with a paw print, a green hat."

Bill does have a catalog, through which he sells 300 or 400 dancers each year. "Once people have been in my booth, they know what my dancers look like, so the catalog doesn't have any photos. It's just a collection of drawings."

Sometimes, he finds that he must also supply photos to customers who live in other parts of the country and have never actually seen his dancers. "I've gotten requests from people in every state in the United States. Sometimes I'll ask these people if they've seen the dancers, and usually they say no. They've just heard about them. So I'll send them some photos

I've taken of some of the characters, and then the customer can say, 'OK. Now I know what this one looks like, so I can imagine what these others look like based on the line drawing.

"A lot of people are surprised that this is the only kind of toy that I make, because normally you'll see 'whirligigs' and 'whimmydiddles' and all kinds of other things. But this is really all I have time to do."

Selling the Line

"Anything that you can do during a show to make noise will help. I know blacksmiths who just pound on their anvil. They're not making anything, but the noise makes folks stop and look."

Eighteen years ago, when he began offering clog dancers for sale, there were few craft shows out there, and there were none of the stature of Winterfair or Yankee Peddler. As a result, Bill found himself selling dancers in small, neighborhood shows.

"The turning point for my business was being accepted into regional and national shows. That makes all the difference in the world. When I was doing neighborhood shows, I might have seen two or three hundred people in a day. Now, when I'm doing the Ann Arbor Street Fair or Yankee Peddler, I might see 60,000 people in a day. And if you're not selling when you see that many people each day, you need to be doing something else."

Bill sees his modest prices—one result of his use of the production-run process—as a key to his success. "My prices are very reasonable. I rarely hear anyone say, 'That's too much money.' In fact, what I usually hear is, 'How can you afford to sell them for that?' That makes me feel good. I enjoy what I do, and I especially enjoy the reaction I get to my work.

"I've always done well at shows. I'm

not dealing with a gender thing or an age thing. The dancers appeal to 4- or 5-year-old children, and they appeal to 95-year-old adults. Men and women; boys and girls.

"Sometimes I don't enjoy the shows. But I keep this in mind: I don't care how miserable this particular experience is. I'm not going to have to be doing this next week and the week after. When the show closes, it's over. Four days is the longest show I do. So I don't enjoy every show I do, but I'm pretty good at making the best of a bad situation.

"I've been in an awful lot of shows where it's too warm or it's raining, and the exhibitors sit in their booths just daring anybody to speak to them. Then they wonder why they're not making any sales. But, hey, I'm out there playing that harmonica, talking to people, and that makes a difference. I never just sit.

"If I'm not playing a harmonica or making a dancer dance, I'm whittling heads. I know I'm going to need them, and its surprising how many conversations that will start. People stop. They want to know what you're doing. Pretty soon, you're demonstrating a dancer, and the people are smiling."

Although he doesn't attempt to maintain an inventory of each of the dancers he makes, he does have, even at the end of the show season, 300 or 400 dancers on hand, a significant representation of the 50 or 60 types he makes. "I like to start the season with a thousand dolls because I may sell almost that many at the Ann Arbor Street Fair."

Planning Production

"I don't time study my operation." He grins. "I might quit if I did."

"When I pick a 2×4 up, I can tell if it's going to make a decent clog dancer." To demonstrate, he lifts a 2×4, estimating its weight. "You can tell its moisture content by its weight. It also needs a certain density." This he estimates by weight and the feel of the wood in his hands.

Before cutting them to length, Bill rips his 2×4s to a bit less than 2 ¼" wide. He makes this measurement, like all of his shop measurements, by eye, without the assist of a rule. "I just move the fence up and say, "Hmm. That looks good.'

His approach to planning a production run is similarly unorthodox. The number of parts he makes in any individual run is not determined by expected sales of a particular dancer, although that is a factor. Instead, as Bill puts it, "A lot is determined by the knots in the wood. When I'm cutting up the initial stock, I start by cutting out the knots. Sometimes, I end up with a 6" piece. Sometimes I end up with a 4" piece. That's when I decide. A short body generally becomes a bird or a mouse. A little longer body becomes a moose or an elephant.

"I do everything by eye. I never measure anything. The thing is you can adjust. There's no reason why my dancers have to be that precise."

While he may make 16 dancers in a production run, they won't all be of the

"I don't time study my operation." He grins. "I might quit if I did."

Bill estimates the length of a body part on a spruce 2×4.

Bill gang cuts the leg notches in eight blocks by passing this entire assembly over the blade, snugging one side against the fence.

same character. Three or four might be tigers, with the remainder being divided among three or four other characters.

"I usually gang cut sixteen bodies, and they will get me through the day pretty easily, because I can only make 10 or 12 a day. To an extent, the number is determined by, for instance, how many dogs'

heads I made the night before. I don't even think in terms of a set number of characters in a particular production run.

"I'll paint the flesh coat on a half a dozen. Then by the time the last one's finished, the first one's ready for a shirt. So then I can paint shirts, and when I'm done with that, I can go back and paint

When seated in the chair on which his right hand now rests, Bill machine sands parts to their finished shape in front of an exhaust fan. Notice under his left hand the compartmentalized tray in which he stores finished arms and legs for his various dancers.

pants on them.

"So I don't really know how long it takes me to do one. Plus, that doesn't take into account how long it takes me to drive into Zanesville to get supplies. It doesn't take into account sanding time and looking for lost tools, that kind of thing.

"More and more people are beginning to realize how much work goes into something like my dancers. Initially, folks didn't know what they were looking at. The oldest show in Ohio is maybe 35 years old, and up until 20 years ago, there just weren't that many craft shows. Now, you can do a show every weekend of the year, so people are beginning to learn."

The Use of the Workstation

Bill's day begins in the shop, where he cuts out and forms the various bodies, arms and legs he will need that day. As the day wears on, he moves to the studio. There, in a room dedicated to the tasks, he makes hats and applies feathers or hair to heads. Then, at another location in that same building, he assembles dancers composed of parts painted the previous day. If necessary, he also does a quick turn at another workstation in that same room, whittling heads with a craft knife.

At noon, he returns to his house and continues to work through his meal. "I paint with one hand while I eat peanut butter and jelly sandwiches with the other."

In the afternoon, he returns to the shop and once again becomes a woodworker, remaining there until 5:30. Then, after supper, he climbs back up the hill to his studio for another round of carving heads and assembling bodies.

Finally, at 8:30 P.M., he goes back down the hill to the house, carrying with him whatever body parts are ready for the application of paint. There, in the front room facing the driveway, he paints, until 11:30 P.M.

As he explains it, the continual migration from one workstation to the next reduces the effects of mental fatigue. "I rarely get bored. This is a great job for someone with attention deficit disorder because you don't have to do any one thing for very long. There's always something else that needs doing."

Bill tapes pairs of arms and legs together prior to cutting notches and tenons. In this manner, he is able to more accurately drill nail holes perpendicular to the sawn faces of those notches and tenons.

At one of several workstations in his shop, Bill drills the nail holes he will later use when assembling the dancers.

At another workstation in his studio, Bill whittles a head. A bucket of heads sits on the floor at his left.

At this workstation, located in Bill's house, he applies paint to the body parts that will eventually become dancers.

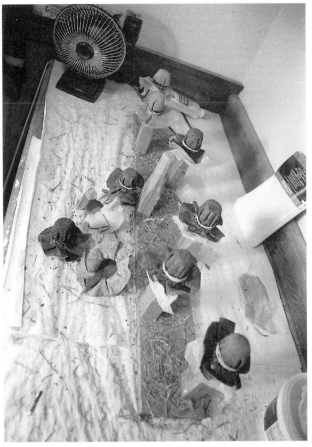

Bits of fabric are dipped into diluted solutions of white glue, then pressed into place over rounded pegs and held there by rubber bands until the glue sets.

At yet another location in his studio, Bill applies hair and hats to the painted dancers.

Here, Bill assembles painted body parts.

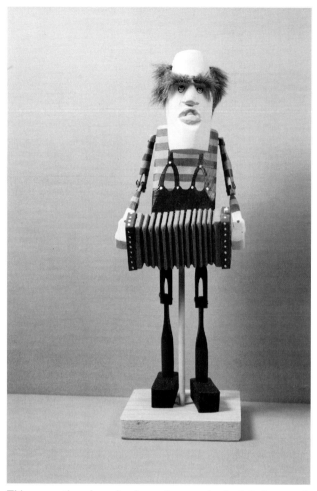

This concertina player has been given a pair of painted suspenders and a fringe of hair.

These two countrywomen are hard at work on a quilt.

Bill labors to give each of his characters a bit of personality. Ears, a couple of carved facial lines and a coat of paint have transformed a handful of wood into a morose dalmatian.

Of all Bill's dancers, this kangaroo with joey and spats is one of the more time-consuming to construct.

CHAPTER EIGHT

WARREN MAY

Finding a Balance

Fashioned primarily from native woods, Warren's dulcimers can be identified by their distinctive sound holes, their textured tuning pegs and their S-shaped tailpieces. Notice the hourdrop shape of the walnut dulcimer. On one side, the body has an hourglass shape, and on the other it has the shape of a teardrop. This combination is one of Warren's innovations.

F O C U S : Warren May's dulcimer-making operation is based on one principle: The best production runs are those that combine the warmth and intimacy of hand detailing and the efficiencies of twentieth-century machine work.

When I arrive at his gallery in downtown Berea, Kentucky, Warren is seated at a long workbench. At his left hand is an array of small hand tools: knife, carving gouges, bits of sandpaper. A nearly completed dulcimer sits on the counter in front of him. Several other dulcimers, executed in a variety of woods, hang on the wall behind him. Bluegrass music is playing, and warm, April sunlight washes into the room through the dozens of tiny panes of glass making up the gallery's north and east walls.

Warren comes around his bench to greet me. We shake hands. I then ask if I can take a few minutes to look at the work on display in the gallery.

A pair of magnificent solid wood highboy armoires—one done in cherry, the other in walnut—face the entrance door. Several of his signature sideboards are positioned in the center of the room, some whose aprons and splashboards have retained their natural, from-the-log edges. Baskets of treenware, made from the scraps left behind during the manufacture of furniture and dulcimers, are arranged in front of the east window. Included among this treenware is a heap of spurtles—stirring utensils I have never before seen.

Finished with my tour of the gallery, I pull an ancient mule-eared chair seated in hickory bark into position in front of Warren's workbench.

He seats himself on a stool behind the bench. He then lifts a rough-cut walnut dulcimer scroll from the bench, turning it so that I can see the wildly figured grain. "This summer we'll make our 10,000th dulcimer, and I'm saving this scroll for one of the commemorative models."

It's been a year and a half since my last visit to Warren's shop, and for several minutes we talk about the changes in his operation since that time. The most noticeable of these is the gallery itself. At the time of my last visit, this storefront gallery was Warren's shop. It was then filled with machinery and benches, all arranged behind a counter that stood near the entrance door. His gallery at that time was a block and a half away, in several connected upstairs rooms.

Warren explains that his shop is now located out in the country near his residence. "All I do here," he gestures at the workbench, "is the handwork."

A man with dark hair and a trim, athletic build enters the gallery. He smiles and waves at Warren. He begins to study the furniture on display. He is clearly impressed. Warren leaves his position behind the bench and walks out to shake hands.

"We do all our own furniture and all our own dulcimers," he explains to the dark-haired man.

"Wow." The man shakes his head in wonder.

Warren brings the man over to my chair to introduce us. He gestures at the man. "He's an electrician, working on the new Wal-Mart. He's been visiting our church."

Warren stands in front of one of his hand-built highboys.

The three of us begin to talk about dulcimers. To demonstrate how easy it is to play the instrument, Warren begins to fret and strum one of the models laid out on his workbench. He then begins to sing.

This is something he does very naturally, without nervous preamble, and his voice is pleasant, his simple singing style perfectly suited to the accompaniment of the dulcimer. The song is a hymn I recognize but can't name. The electrician then steps closer to Warren, and he, too, begins to sing. Their voices fill the gallery.

Growing Up in Woodworking

"As a boy, I worked in a nonelectrified shop with hand tools. And still today, I texture pieces with spokeshaves and hand planes."

As one of ten children growing up on a farm in Carroll County, Kentucky, Warren was raised with the idea that useful things could be made from wood. If, for example, his mother needed a rolling pin, his father simply split stock from a firewood billet, then shaped that stock into a rolling pin with a drawknife.

"I still have a few things of my dad's," Warren explains. "He was quite a woodworker. He could split shingles. He could carve.

"And both my grandfathers made furniture. I have a tiny milk stool that one of them made from walnut. He whittled the parts in front of the fire, then fastened it together with wooden pegs."

After a childhood spent in the family workshop, Warren took his interest in woodworking to Eastern Kentucky University to prepare for a career as a high school shop teacher. "There, at Eastern, I had a very experienced and sage woodworking teacher, Ralph Whalin. He was classical in his approach. His students learned to do things properly, and while we didn't always know why we did things in a certain way, we did learn good construction."

It was there, too, that he had his first significant contact with the dulcimer. "Homer Ledford, from Winchester, Kentucky, is probably Kentucky's senior dulcimer maker. He works primarily by himself. He's invented the dulcitar, the duclibro: These are hybrids, combining the dulcimer with other instruments. Today, he's one of the finest musical instrument craftsmen and woodcarvers in the United States.

"Homer came from Tennessee, went to Berea College, then to Eastern Kentucky some years before me, and one of his dulcimers was in the office of my department chairman the whole four years I attended Eastern."

Although Warren enjoyed his contact with his students during his time as a high school shop teacher, it wasn't long before he found himself considering other career possibilities. "There were influences to leave teaching and go into industry because teaching didn't pay very much." Warren then began a woodworking business that not only supplemented his teaching income but, and just as important, provided him with an outlet for his creative energies.

His first pieces were furniture, reproductions done in the Queen Anne style. Some he built for his own use. Others were sold to friends and co-workers. All were built in the high school shop in which he taught. During this period, he was in that shop almost continuously, working with his students by day (and some evenings) and on his own work at night.

"But it wasn't until I began making dulcimers in my third or fourth year of teaching that I really began to sell my work."

"As a boy, I worked in a nonelectrified shop with hand tools. And still today, I texture pieces with spokeshaves and hand planes."

Building the Business

"At the time I quit teaching and became a full-time maker of dulcimers, I had no experience with production work."

If Warren had been born in some other part of the country, it's quite possible that his 25-year association with the dulcimer—an association which has shaped both his professional and personal life—would never have occurred.

But he was born and raised in Kentucky, and that geographical circumstance inevitably brought him into contact with this most traditional of mountain instruments. Warren explains, "Kentucky is probably the most important location for traditional, Appalachian dulcimers. One of the reasons for this is Jean Ritchie."

"Jean Ritchie's music has been featured on numerous KET [The Kentucky Network, Kentucky Educational Television] shows and on Bill Moyer's *Amazing Grace*. She took the dulcimer from eastern Kentucky, where it was isolated, to England, where she worked as a Fulbright Scholar. She researched and wrote the first dulcimer book. She brought the dulcimer out of the mountains and made it a viable American folk instrument."

The work, then, of Jean Ritchie, Homer Ledford and others created an environment in which a maker of Kentucky dulcimers, like Warren May, might succeed in.

However, the first musical instrument Warren attempted to build was not a dulcimer but a plywood balalaika modeled on one appearing in the movie *Doctor Zhivago*. "That instrument didn't play very well because I didn't have it fretted properly. I had had no musical training at all, and I didn't understand any of the theory of music."

Soon after the construction of the balalaika, Warren began work on his first dulcimer. "I just started cutting out parts and pieces. I had no plans. I had seen a kit in Gatlinburg, but I couldn't afford to buy it."

After selling that first dulcimer, Warren taught for another five years, during which time he sold another 175. Then, in 1977, with no experience in mass production, Warren and his wife, Frankye, (who manages their gallery) quit their jobs as teachers, cashed in their retirement plans, and Warren became a full-time maker of dulcimers.

Much careful planning preceded the move, beginning just after Christmas of their last year in the classroom. Warren started by purchasing equipment. One of his first major acquisitions was a Belsaw planer. They purchased other machines at Sears, transactions made easier by his intended career change. "When I was a schoolteacher, I had a $200 credit limit. But when I told them I was quitting my job and going into business for myself, they said, 'Oh, then you've got $2,000 worth of credit.'"

Warren and Frankye also began what turned out to be a lengthy search for a town where their business might flourish. They considered Asheville, North Carolina, which at that time had an active craft community. They decided, however, that it was an area more suitable for retirees than young families. They also looked at several towns in Colorado: Boulder, Denver, Fort Collins. "It was an exciting area. Crafts were catching on. They had warehouses there that craftspeople could rent to use as shop space. People were making rustic mountain furniture. One of my friends was making bronze belt buckles. But it was too windy, too cold and maybe too commercial."

Eventually, they settled on Berea,

"At the time I quit teaching and became a full-time maker of dulcimers, I had no experience with production work."

> "A guitar maker called me and said he wanted to make a really fine dulcimer. I told him to build a hundred and throw the first 99 away."

Kentucky. In part, they chose Berea because it was close to home and within easy driving distance of their families and a weekend cabin they'd built on some land a student's father had given to Warren. But there was another, even more important, reason for their choice. "It was because of the quality of the craftwork being done in Berea. Since 1900, Berea College had been holding craft fairs, and by the 1970s, there were a number of craftsmen already at work here, including several woodworkers. Basically, Berea denoted quality. To sell here, work had to be the very finest examples of workmanship and artistry. "Now," Warren explains, "there must be 35 artists' studios and shops in town, and these are all people who make their living with their hands."

Planning Production

"A guitar maker called me and said he wanted to make a really fine dulci-

mer. I told him to build a hundred and throw the first 99 away."

A great woodworking craftsperson who decides to make a single dulcimer can make an instrument that is both beautiful and playable. However, no matter how meticulously it was crafted that instrument will never play any better than the one on which it's modeled. Improvements in playability can be achieved only through experimentation, a process requiring the construction of many dulcimers. Warren May has made many dulcimers and in the process has learned a great deal about how the playability of the instrument can be enhanced.

One characteristic he has experimented with is the overall shape of the instrument. Warren explains, "There are two traditional shapes for the dulcimer: hourglass and teardrop. The teardrop is harder to make, and for years we just couldn't get that kind of dulcimer to sound right. They were interesting, and some people wanted that traditional shape, but we kept working and working,

Warren feeds a fret board past a gang saw designed to cut the nut and 15 fret slots at the same time.

and we just couldn't get them to sound right.

"So one day about 11 years ago, we laid an hourglass top on one side and a teardrop top on the other and we said, 'Just for fun, let's make one that's half-and-half.'

"Well, we did it, and that dulcimer sounded better than either the hourglass or the teardrop. We called it the 'hour-drop'—that's my own coined name for it—so we immediately dropped the teardrop.

"This taught us that we could improve the tone of the instrument. Rather than just making them, we could look at what we were doing and improve the musical quality."

The fret board is another feature that Warren has manipulated to improve the instrument's playability. "Over the years, we have learned that the fret board is the heart of the instrument. We learned that getting the fret board perfectly straight or slightly bowed down—this is done in the first gluing operation, one that stays with you from start to finish—is critical. We also learned to thin our fret board down, going from ⅜″ walls to ¼″ walls. (We also thinned down all the internal construction of the dulcimer, which made it sound a lot better).

"Then we found that if we used lighter selections of wood for the fret board, we got better tone. We looked for wood that had heartwood on one side and sapwood on the other, and we used that material for the fret board, turning it so that the light wood (the sapwood) was on the bottom and the heartwood was on the top."

His experimentation with materials has given him firsthand knowledge of the acoustical properties of the various species of wood used for instrument tops and bottoms. "I used to wonder why Martin used rosewood in their guitars and Gibson used mahogany in theirs.

This detail of the fret saw shows the blades peeking up through the sliding table.

Well, in making rosewood dulcimers, I think I learned the answer: Mahogany is a soft wood, and rosewood is very hard. Martins, then, made of rosewood, have a very strong, bright sound. Gibsons, made of mahogany, have a hummy, personal, warm sound. That's why Gibsons won't play bluegrass very well. But Martins have that bite that bluegrass requires."

He has also experimented with the appearance of his dulcimers. "I started doing heart shapes and hummingbirds for sound holes. Then one day, I decided to use a knot hole for a sound hole. I thought I was being so brave—and now, that knothole has become one of my trademarks."

While many of the signature features of the Warren May dulcimer are the result of his own thinking, others evolved due to input from friends. Warren tells this story to explain: "In my last year of teaching, the principal of my school, who had been working in gun shops, came to me and said, 'Why do you make a square tailpiece on your dulcimers? It doesn't go with the rest of your instrument.' So I went over to the band saw and cut out my little S-shaped tailpiece, and that tailpiece completed my instrument. Since that day, I have not made a single square tailpiece."

"I think wood-working is much easier and more accurate than it used to be, thanks to technology, although we never tried to make things even easier by making our dulcimer fit a machine operation."

In spite of his experimentation, the Warren May dulcimer remains a very traditional musical instrument. For example, the fact that it is made of wood is a very important consideration. "We use the wood as the key design element, with very little added ornamentation." He has also preserved some of the distinguishing visual characteristics of traditional instruments. "We do have in ours the features of the Kentucky dulcimer: the scroll, the carved keys, the bead around the top and bottom."

Warren points to his vast body of experience with this instrument as one of the keys to his success. "We've been able to refine both the construction methods and the tone, but that's only come about because we've been able to consistently build the same instrument year after year. This is our 25th year."

"I think woodworking is much easier and more accurate than it used to be, thanks to technology, although we never tried to make things even easier by making our dulcimer fit a machine operation."

Warren admits that the methods he first used in the construction of his dulcimers were crude and sometimes dangerous. "I was making my thin wood by planing 1″ boards down to ⅛″. I didn't know about resawing. Then I started sawing my thin wood on the table saw with a carbide blade, sawing it on the top and bottom, sometimes sawing it all the way off. This was so dangerous that I would only do it late at night, when nobody else was there to distract me.

"Then someone gave me an old meat saw, and we began to use that, with a 1″ blade, to resaw thin wood." At first, Warren struggled to make this meat saw perform accurate work. Then a salesman suggested a different type of band saw blade. "He gave us some Lenox flexback, thin-kerf band saw blades as free samples. And they are wonderful. That one little change helped to refine many of our processes."

His methods for sanding this thin wood have also undergone a number of changes. "At first, I sanded each piece down with a Stanley portable belt sander. Then I began to take this resawn stuff to the college [Berea College] and

The forms used to bend dulcimer sides hang on the shop wall.

have it sanded on their equipment at $150 per hour. Then finally, when I got an order from the Smithsonian for a hundred dulcimers, I ordered a Custer drum sander to sand this thin wood."

The fret board is the heart of any stringed instrument, and in order for that instrument to play well, the frets must be accurately aligned. "When I started, I had to mark each one from my master fret pattern, scribe the cuts with a knife and saw them with a modified coping saw blade. It would take all day long to do ten fret boards.

"Very early on, I realized that the first thing I needed to do was find a faster way to saw the frets. We have a local retired missionary who is a great wood mechanic, Ursal Kindel. He's helped several of the area woodworkers resolve problems. I took the fret-sawing problem to him, and he helped me grind some milling machine blades down and mount them on a half-inch arbor. He then made a sliding table that sits on drawer slides to pass the fret boards over this gang saw. And I'm still using this saw, which

saws the nut and 15 fret slots at the same time.

"Over the years we've made a number of improvements to this saw: adding a larger motor; substituting a larger, dampened arbor; changing the position of the frets [for the more accurate playing of the instrument]. Now, I can saw two or three fret boards per minute."

The fabrication of tuning keys is another process that has undergone extensive refinement in Warren's shop. "I use Brazilian rosewood for the keys. We band saw it to ½″ stock, mark it out with a white pencil, and band saw the profiles. Then we turn it in a lathe, using a little chuck head that we made. We then turn the stock to a rough size and sand the shaft to a taper. Finally we texture the top of each key with a Dremel tool."

Gluing up dulcimer bodies is perhaps the fussiest and most labor-intensive process in the construction of the dulcimer. For years, Warren did this work himself, patiently bending the sides into place, then fixing them there between the top and bottom with a great number

PHOTO 2. Heckman then levels the top edges of the dulcimer sides with a block of wood covered in sandpaper. Notice that the outside cauls of the gluing mold are pressed up tight against the dulcimer sides, being held there by the small blocks of wood turned lengthwise between the cauls and the stop-blocks.

PHOTO 3. Heckman applies a bead of glue to the top edge of the dulcimer sides.

PHOTO 4. He then carefully positions the top.

PHOTO 5. At this point, the top half of the mold is moved into place. Notice the dozens of spring-loaded bolts passing through the mold top. The heads of these bolts will apply clamping pressure all around the dulcimer top while the glue cures.

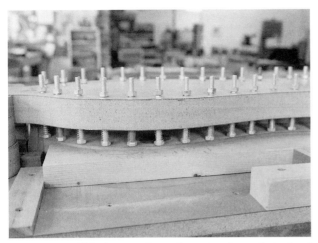

PHOTO 6. This close-up shows the springs beneath the head of each bolt used in the mold top. These springs make it possible to apply pressure gently.

PHOTO 7. After the glue securing the dulcimer top has cured, the dulcimer body is inverted so the bottom can be glued in place in a similar mold.

PHOTO 8. Notice the clamp under Heckman's left hand. The design of the gluing mold permits this single clamp to apply pressure at each of the dozens of bolt head locations around the circumference of the gluing mold.

PHOTO 9. This photo shows several of the molds used in Warren's shop. The mold on the right is clamping a dulcimer top in place.

A custom-ground, flush-cut laminate bit is used to shape the bead on the dulcimer tops and bottoms.

time we did get them refined. They're large, spring-loaded and covered in Formica. Now, with the molds, one of my employees can glue up six or seven dulcimers each day."

One distinguishing characteristic of Warren's dulcimers is a bead cut on the lapped edges of the top and bottom, edges which follow the dulcimer's serpentine sides. At one point, Warren formed this bead by hand, using carving tools and sandpaper. "If you're working with a figured wood, like curly maple or walnut, it's just about impossible to carve that bead all around the top and bottom without tearing out at least one chip.

"With a little experimentation, I was able to use a flush-cut laminate bit for this operation. I had to hire someone to cut a groove in the carbide. Then we had to trim the shank down to fit in a Dremel tool. Later, we redesigned it so that we can use a ¼" Makita collet. Now I trim the bead all around all four sides of a dulcimer in less than a minute, leaving only a little in the corners that we have to shape by hand."

In addition to sanding the resawn

of small clamps. Now, however, Warren uses sets of custom-designed gluing molds. "Before we had the molds, I was spending three or four months out of the year gluing dulcimer sides in, holding them in place with a bunch of spring clamps, and I was getting tired of it.

"It took us about three tries to work up our dulcimer molds, which allow us to glue together the fret board, the bottom and the top all at one time. That last

This Fein sander with a modified head can even be used to smooth the interior surfaces of the scroll cavity.

Warren uses a pantograph to guide a router that makes the inscribed cut on the sides of the scroll.

Notice the line of scrolls near the bottom of the photo. These scrolls illustrate several of the 20 manufacturing steps each scroll requires. The scroll on the right has been sawn to the approximate size. The notches that will later receive the ends of the dulcimer sides have been cut. To the left of that scroll is one showing the work of the pantograph-directed router. The next scroll to the left has been drilled to receive the tuning keys. Finally, the block on the extreme left has been profiled on the band saw.

stock prior to cutting out parts, the finished dulcimers must be sanded through a variety of grits prior to assembly." We used to hand sand with rubber blocks. At one time we started with 50-grit. Then we switched to 80, then to 100, working up through the grits, all by hand.

"Then one of my employees saw a Fein sander at a show, and they had just reduced the price from $300 to $200, which made it even more attractive. I bought the Fein sander and put on a piece of rough paper, and it just burrowed into the wood, so I thought, 'This isn't going to work.' Then we put finer sandpaper on it, and it worked fine. Later, we found out we could make our own sanding heads to the shapes we needed. So we made one with a little head that fit between the beads, and now we do all the sanding with that tool."

In general, Warren recommends quality cutting tools. "It's a good investment to buy better quality sandpaper, router bits and saw blades. For example we use thin-kerf, carbide saw blades, which are much safer and easier to use. You can feed 2″ [5.1cm] stock with just a push stick. Another example is the sticky paper we use on our Fein sanders. We found that by buying the very best 3M paper we can cut one small piece and sand an entire dulcimer. These little things make a difference."

His reliance on production-run methods have paid a perhaps unexpected dividend: He now has the freedom to do more experimentation and more handwork. "I do the beginning, the fretting. I do all the final adjustments to make each dulcimer not only a craft item but also a fine musical instrument.

"Although we've done a lot of things to make the dulcimer better, it's not like we've changed the design of the instrument to fit this automatic milling machine. You know we could have our scrolls made at a furniture factory. We could have sound holes cut with laser etching. But we don't do that. It's still my craft. I have to be able to say that I made it."

Increasing Efficiency

"For 19 years, we gave away boxes and boxes of rips and cutoffs that we'd marked as firewood. Now we're using all that material."

When Warren talks about his operation, he hammers away at the notion of efficiency, and in a production shop that can mean many things. On one level, it simply means working faster, which can be achieved by both improved work methods and improved manual skills. "We started out very simply, hand cutting every part and piece of the dulcimer. Then, the need arose for faster and more efficient production. When I started, I could make about a dulcimer a day. Believe it or not, they still require about a day per instrument, but now I have two employees whose work also results in a dulcimer per man-day."

On another level, efficiency means maximizing the use of material. In this regard, he has recently changed his approach to scrap. "We're also totally recycling our wood, turning all of our scrap into low-end items [boxes, treenware, etc.]. We collect the material in boxes: boxes of stir sticks, boxes of spurtles. We're using the scraps from our dulcimer scrolls to make jam spoons. Other scraps are used to make cutting boards, boxes, whatever we can make. Then we make a dozen here or a dozen there.

"The prices on these items are as little as $3.50 for a small condiment spreader. In this way, we're able to totally fill up our time with productive work. Now we know that we can make fifty, sixty dollars worth of items in an hour. Any given employee can do that. Now we work to maximum capacity."

Efficiency also involves the proper matching of craftsman to task. Some operations Warren still insists on performing himself. Others are performed by his employees who have themselves become highly skilled craftsmen. "We share. We all do different things. We all work to our maximum skill level. We want to get to the point where we're each making pieces at our best level of productivity."

Recently, Warren has begun to streamline the list of dulcimers he offers for sale. This change, too, was dictated by the need for ever greater efficiency. "We've refined out the dulcimer models that people didn't want: for example, maple. We're just now finishing out some of our parts and pieces, mixing that maple with walnut. Even though we were using beautiful bird's-eye and curly maple, it didn't compare to really nice walnut or cherry in tone.

"At one time, I was building forty-some different models and combinations of woods. I was using five or six different scroll stocks, and each scroll requires over 20 different operations. Soon all our scrolls will be made out of poplar, walnut or cherry (which is the most traditional).

"In general, we're eliminating all tropical woods—mahogany, lacewood—and we're going to focus on native woods: poplar, walnut, cherry, butternut."

Warren smiles. "Although there are exceptions. I just got a cache of 40-year-old Brazilian rosewood from Rude Osolink [a nationally known turner also from Berea]. The stock is only ⅜" thick, but we can resaw that one time and get book-matched pieces. We're using walnut fret boards, tailpieces and scrolls with that rosewood. It's making some gorgeous instruments."

Perhaps the most important element in the efficiency equation is quality control. It's not enough to perform work quickly; work must also be performed accurately. "We are all responsible for quality control. Each man either ensures the quality of each detail at his point in the operation or he flags the detail so I can

> "For 19 years, we gave away boxes and boxes of rips and cutoffs that we'd marked as firewood. Now we're using all that material."

look it over later. Every employee has the responsibility for making every dulcimer just as fine as it can be."

Running the Business

"Our kids are prepared to go out and be competitive. They've seen their mom and dad work together in a woodworking business—not just a craft shop."

From the start, Warren and Frankye tried to conduct themselves in a businesslike manner. "We weren't thinking that if I sell one dulcimer I can buy a set of tires, or if I sell a chair I can buy a stove. I think that's not a good way to go into business, although a lot of craftspeople working out of their homes operate with that philosophy."

In the beginning, they tried several different approaches to the problem of selling their work at acceptable prices. "We did a few craft shows, but we were never show people. We tried wholesaling and soon found out that we couldn't get enough out of our items to make it work. Both the furniture and the dulcimers involve far too much handwork to be profitable at wholesale prices.

"That's why we no longer do custom work. It isn't profitable. Now we build a piece as we have time and materials."

Today, nearly all that Warren makes is sold directly to the public out of his gallery in downtown Berea.

"One of the reasons that we've been successful is that we've tried to make our craftwork more of a business. I don't mean that we just make what sells. We try, instead, to make nice items that will sell. What we've found is that we had to make the most profitable things. In order to make a better living, we had to prioritize, to focus on those things that make the most profit.

"When we started, our kids were small, but we knew they'd be successful in school. We knew that someday we'd need money to put them through college, and we've been able to provide them with a lifestyle that's a little better than that provided by the typical backyard craftsperson."

Finding a Balance

Machine work, although noisy and dirty, is very efficient. In an hour, one person of limited skill can feed hundreds of feet of resawn stock through a wide-belt sander, stock that it would take days to surface using traditional hand tools.

Some craftspeople, seduced by this efficiency, design to accommodate the capabilities of machine tools. Warren May takes a different approach.

Warren looks for a balance, setting speed on one side of the scale and hand detailing on the other, using machinery to perform the brute work of ripping, crosscutting and thicknessing, but reserving hand tools for the delicate work of providing his dulcimers with the kind of tactile and visual appeal that have characterized his work for over 25 years.

"Our kids are prepared to go out and be competitive. They've seen their mom and dad work together in a woodworking business—not just a craft shop."

CHAPTER NINE

JUDY DITMER

The Power of Acceptance

No two of Judy's earrings are exactly alike.

FOCUS: Although she works in production runs numbering in the hundreds, no two pieces of Judy Ditmer's turned wooden jewelry are alike. She achieves this variety through the scrupulous application of one principle: The craftsperson must remain open to the design possibilities inherent in the color and figure of the wood emerging at the lathe.

Judy Ditmer is standing in a light rain the first time I see her. It's November and there's a mat of wet leaves on her driveway. The air is cool and crisp. With a wave of one hand, Judy directs our vehicle back toward a parking area near her shop in Piqua, Ohio.

Although we've talked on the phone a half dozen times, and although I've read her two books, *Turning Wooden Jewelry* and *Basic Bowl Turning*, I haven't yet had an opportunity to speak to her face-to-face.

As I watch her through the back window of my photographer's Jeep Cherokee, I notice a hitch in Judy's step. Her stride is uncertain, labored. I recall that, on the phone, she's mentioned chronic health problems and surgery.

I exit the Jeep. Judy and I shake hands. She offers a warm smile. She's wearing dark work pants, a blue turtleneck and a purple insulated vest. Her hair is slightly disarrayed, as if she's been working in the shop. I notice she has the compact body of a woman not unaccustomed to physical labor.

I ask if she's feeling well.

She shakes her head. "I was hoping to feel better today. In fact, I almost called you to cancel."

I ask her what's wrong.

"Dizziness." She shrugs ruefully. "My balance isn't good today, and I'm very tired."

I ask her if she feels up to the interview.

The warm smile flashes on and off. "Sure. Once I get moving, I'll be all right."

Examining the Shop

"When I was a kid, my friends and I would have these fantasies about what our lives would be like when we were grown up. We drew them out on paper, and when I drew mine, I always had a darkroom, a workshop, a photo studio and a painting studio."

Judy offers to help us with our gear. Arms loaded with photography equipment, she leads us around the garage at the rear of her home to her shop, a shed-roofed addition extending out from the back wall of the garage. Opening the door, she invites us inside.

A large short-bed lathe stands dead ahead rising from a mountain of shavings laid down in multicolored layers. I see dark shavings at the base of the mountain (walnut perhaps), then a lighter color mounded over the dark (perhaps maple), then frosting the top, a layer of pink, which I later learn is pink ivorywood. Taken together, these layers constitute a kind of geological record of recent turning activity.

Scattered around the room are other stationary power tools: a drill press, a band saw, bench grinders, and in the center of the room is a Shopsmith set up for spindle turning. Bits of wood, rough turnings and tools are heaped everywhere, piled onto benches and tables. A layer of sanding dust clings to every surface. This shop isn't a display model. This is one in which a real craftsperson is doing real work.

After we put down our equipment, Judy takes us on a tour, leading us through the garage into the house. In the kitchen, we're ambushed by cats who soundlessly appear from several directions. Judy introduces us, but the cats are unimpressed, curling once around our ankles, then slipping off to other, more important affairs.

Art is everywhere in Judy's home: framed and hung on the walls, placed on shelves, even in the bathroom. Much of it is wooden: turned pieces, carved pieces and pieces that appear to have

> "When I was a kid, my friends and I would have these fantasies about what our lives would be like when we were grown up. We drew them out on paper, and when I drew mine, I always had a darkroom, a workshop, a photo studio and a painting studio."

"I went to a turning conference in 1985 in Gatlinburg, and I was just blown out of the water. I said, 'Whoa. This is why I'm so bored making furniture.' "

Judy looks for a variety of color and end-grain pattern when selecting stock for a run of jewelry. (The keys are shown to indicate scale.)

been both turned and carved. Some Judy identifies as her own work. Other art is the work of friends.

In addition to the wooden pieces, I see drawings, prints, fabric art and ceramics.

The last area we visit is the basement. Bright and well lit, this is where she assembles the earrings that make up the biggest share of her yearly sales. This is also where she conducts business. I sit at her desk; she sits at her worktable. We settle in to talk.

Developing Skills

"I went to a turning conference in 1985 in Gatlinburg, and I was just blown out of the water. I said, 'Whoa. This is why I'm so bored making furniture.' "

The 1950s were a different time.

Leave It to Beaver and *Father Knows Best* dominated the popular consciousness, informing viewers by example that little girls worked in the kitchen with their mothers, while the workshop was the domain of little boys and their fathers. Rarely was this division of labor discussed. It was simply a matter of expectation, as if this policy somehow reflected natural law.

For this reason, even though she had an interest in woodworking as a child, Judy found it almost impossible to get even the very rough instruction that a little boy of the same era might have expected. "It was very difficult for me to get into the field because I never had a speck of encouragement. My own grandfather: when I asked him to teach me some woodworking, he just laughed."

Not surprisingly then, Judy's interest in working with her hands took a different course: the fine arts. There it was expected that girls would manipulate media. There she found no gender bias against the use of tools, although in the art studio, the tools were brushes and pencils instead of the saws and planes she would have used in the workshop.

However, because of a lack of formal training, her first post-high-school experiences in the field of fine arts were not what she had expected. She explains, "When I got out of high school, I went to art school, the Kansas City Art Institute, and had a horrible experience. I was there with all these people who had gone to fine arts high schools in New York City and places like that. They had done metal sculpture and printmaking, and I had come from this little high school, Tipp City, with one art teacher for the whole school system. Most of my time in the art room had come during study hall, when I worked on my own with no teacher there.

"I just hadn't had the kind of preparation I needed. That was real difficult. I left Kansas City after one term.

"Also, I'm not at all academically inclined. Although I've had a couple of years of college, I don't fit in there. I don't like it. I think it's tiresome to have to follow somebody else's directions."

She began working wood as a hobby in the early 1980s. "I started building stuff in, maybe, 1982. At that time, I was doing a wholesale natural foods business, selling to co-ops and natural food stores. I did a trucking run every other week, and in between I had a large amount of time with not too many things I had to do. I bought a Shopsmith and started learning how to do some stuff. I started doing workbenches for the shop. I didn't really know what I was doing.

"I give a lot of credit to the Shopsmith people. They never laughed at me. Admittedly, they were selling me machines, but they were really great. They answered questions, gave me help. They had these little sawdust sessions, these little free things you could go to in the evening."

Shortly after her purchase of a Shopsmith, Judy began to do small commission pieces. "I had a couple of people say, 'Can you make me a such-and-such?' And I said, 'Sure.'

"In 1986, my co-op business ended, for various reasons. I then worked about six months in a cabinet shop. I was spraying lacquer. Nobody else wanted to do it. I was really good at it, so I was stuck with it. One day, I was in the spray room in this metal building, and it was maybe 95° out. I had on my mask and my goggles and my apron. I was spraying this huge roomful of cabinets."

Judy laughs as she tells the story. "I had what I call a *depiphany*. An *epiphany* is when you realize how wonderful the universe really is. A *depiphany* is when you realize how awful and meaningless your life really is.

"I realized that I couldn't keep doing that. It was driving me crazy. The boss was a nice guy, but I was not getting paid very well. So I thought, 'Well, if I'm going to be this broke, I'm going to be this broke working for myself.'

"I just quit. This is not the story of the yuppie with the wonderful job who decides he wants to go grow apples in the country. I didn't have a wonderful job. What did I have to lose?"

On her band saw, Judy cuts an X into the end grain of each piece of turning stock. The spurs on her lathe's drive center will fit into these cuts.

Building the Business

"I think a person could make $100,000 a year in craftwork, although I couldn't. I would be too bored by the things I would have to do to make that kind of money," says Ditmer.

Craftwork isn't like conventional employment. There are no employee softball leagues. There are no office Christmas parties. There are no co-workers who can offer consolation at the water cooler when something has gone terribly wrong.

With a roughing gouge, Judy turns each piece of turning stock into a cylinder.

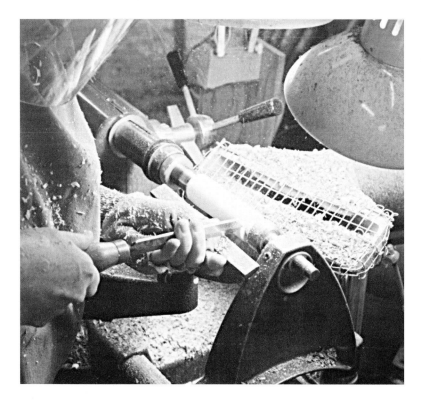

She then switches to a parting tool and cuts a short spigot on one end of the turning stock. This spigot will later be fit into a hole cut into a lathe-mounted waste block.

The turning stock for a run of jewelry has been rendered into cylinders. Notice the short spigot on one end of each cylinder.

And there's no time clock.

"When I'm getting ready for a show, I work ridiculously long hours because I never have stuff done that I want to get done. And after a show, I always crash out for a couple of days and don't work at all.

"I guess my ideal schedule would be this: I'd get up early, and I'd work in the shop for five, six, seven hours. Then I'd come in, and I'd take a break. I'd fix some

dinner, clean the house or do errands. Then I'd come down to my office and work—you know, photography, applications, that sort of thing."

Although she finds that the lifestyle of a craftsperson suits her personality, she cautions others to think carefully before they take it up. "People have this fantasy of quitting their jobs and working as artists, but I tell them, 'If you have a choice, don't do it.'

"I didn't really have a choice."

She gestures at the house around her. "Although for me, this lifestyle works really well. I have this big house, and I have my cats. I have my darkroom. I have my workshop."

The individual who works in an office or a factory is paid a wage from the first day of employment, even for those days that individual spends learning the job. However, for people who choose a career in craftwork, there are no paychecks during the weeks and months spent learning the craft.

"For the first several years, I didn't make any money. I did some shows. I also had some sewing customers—I used to do that kind of work—and my mother helped me out because I'd been so sick. She helped me out financially so I was able to limp along for a couple of years until I started making money.

"And my lifestyle was pretty marginal. When I first started, I was in a rented house. My rent was about a $175, which we can hardly imagine now."

Judy laughs. "I got kicked out of that house when the owner found out I was doing woodwork in one of the rooms, although I was always very careful not to do anything that would damage the house."

To be successful in the craft field, one must define a marketing niche. For some, that niche may consist entirely of retail shows. For others, it may be a close association with a handful of art galleries. Judy relies on a combination of wholesale accounts and a handful of retail shows.

"Wholesale is the core of my business. I also do the Rosen Show in February in Philadelphia. That's my big one.

"I have done more retail this year, just trying to pay off medical debt. I enjoy retail shows if I only do three or four a year, but if I have to do them all summer and all fall, it's really brutal. It's very demanding physically, and, of course, I haven't been well physically. It's also real draining emotionally because at a show where you just have a general population, they don't know anything about your work."

The sexism that Judy encountered as a child when she attempted to learn woodworking can, even today, surface at a retail show. "There can be a lot of stupid questions—you know, 'Did you make this?' I'll be sitting there with my name tag on and my name on the booth, and people will look around for the guy.

"I think it's changing. There are several professional female turners that I personally know or know of their work. Now if you go to a woodturning conference, maybe 20 percent of the people there are women, although not all of them have serious aspirations about selling their work and making a living."

Judy's friends have always been supportive of her decision to make a living as a woodworker. "In fact, most of my friends now are people I know from doing shows." She hesitates, then continues reflectively. "It's kind of a strange life. I don't have kids. I don't go to church, and I don't work here in town. So I don't know many people here in town."

Because of the skills she's acquired through countless hours at the lathe, Judy has been offered a number of opportunities to share her hard-won knowledge. "I've done a fair amount of teach-

This faceplate-mounted waste block will hold each piece of turning stock as it is rendered into discs.

ing. I don't like to do it more than maybe two to four times a year because I want to enjoy it, and being on the road is really tiring."

Although she has taught mostly at locations other than her home in Dayton, Ohio, she has "done two or three things here. A club from Cincinnati came up one time. They wanted to see my shop, and that's great. But mostly I travel to teach. In fact, I got to go to Utah this year, which was terrific. After the conference, I rented a car and took five days to travel around Utah."

Judy isn't optimistic about her chances of ever selling her work for prices significantly higher than those she now charges. "I think there is a limit to what people will pay for certain categories of items. As far as the high-priced, one-of-a-kind turnings—which I don't do very many of because they are so hard to sell—the collector's market is very, very small. There are very, very few people who buy that kind of work.

"So in order to work and make money, you've got to break out of the collector's market. If you're out there just selling wood turnings, that's going to be very difficult. But if you can, sell turnings that

> "To carve an elephant, you take a block of wood and cut away everything that's not part of the elephant."

aren't really turnings—by that I mean jewelry, things like that, like my earrings. Even though they're turned, the people who buy them aren't buying turnings; they're buying earrings. And these are people who already buy earrings. The only question is whether or not they buy mine. But if I'm selling a sculptural piece, well, many people don't even know what that is."

Planning Production

"To carve an elephant, you take a block of wood and cut away everything that's not part of the elephant."

"I think the thing about turning that is most important to me is this: The designing and the making of the piece can be totally integrated in time. This is almost never true when you're building furniture. Even when you're making new and innovative pieces of furniture, there is a considerable separation between the design and the making. With turning, those processes are completely integrated."

Sometimes Judy begins with a plan based upon the characteristics of the piece of wood she is about to turn. At other times, she mounts the wood in her lathe and lets the design happen.

"Stephen Jay Gould, the archaeologist and teacher who writes a column for *Natural History* magazine, has discussed a popular misconception about the work of archaeology and physical anthropology: the idea that you can take one bone and from that you can postulate the whole creature. He says that's not really true.

"Even though that's not really true in archaeology, it is, nevertheless, an interesting idea with application in my work. Sometimes, I'll start with the foot of the bowl. Maybe I'll start with a curved foot, and it's like that mythical one bone from which the archaeologist postulates everything. Once you've turned that foot, the entire bowl has been decided.

"Sometimes, I put little tool cuts along the side. If I mess that up and I have to turn the sides down to clean up the mistake, I have to go back and redo the foot and redo the rim because it doesn't work anymore. Just taking off that little bit of material changes everything. A really successful piece has the feel that it works together very tightly.

"There's a strong sense that within that block of wood is the final surface and that when I reach that final surface, I should know it. I'm listening and watching for that moment when the final surface emerges.

"I think that's why I was so not at home in the academic world. There, you're supposed to be able to postulate all this stuff ahead of time, and that isn't how it works for me at all. For me, it's almost totally intuitive."

Her devotion to her craft has involved Judy in some lively discussions both in the flesh and on the pages of *American Woodturner* magazine.

"Some turners think there's only one right way to do everything, and that's the way it should be done. But I think there

Beginning with the diameter of the smallest spigot in this particular production run, Judy transfers spigot diameter to the waste block with a pair of metal calipers. Notice that it is only the spur on the left which touches (and marks) the waste block. If the spur on the right were to touch the waste block, the tool would be jerked from her hand.

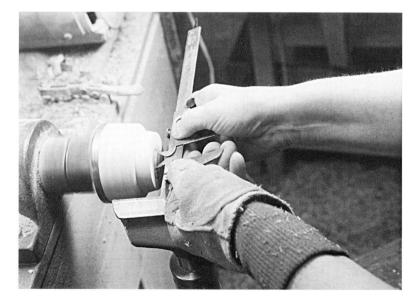

are ways that are easier than other ways and there are ways that are more fun than other ways. I say if it works for you and you're happy with it, fine.

"For instance, sharpening jigs are a big issue. I used to be unalterably opposed to sharpening jigs because it's really easy for me to sharpen since I've had a lot of practice at it. And I'm better at stuff that's not so rigid because I have a kind of intuitive approach to everything. But for guys who turn on weekends and maybe not every weekend, who don't really understand how the tool should look in the first place let alone how to get it there, the jig can be a really useful thing. But I personally would hate to rely on it. Besides which, no matter how adaptable the jig, sooner or later you're going to need to change this edge a little bit so you can do this thing that's a little bit different than you've ever done before.

"Sanding is another controversial issue. You can either turn a bowl really, really clean with a tool or you can sand it into submission. I enjoy cutting with the tool a lot more than I do sanding, and overall, I think it's better to learn how to finish a surface with a tool. But if some guy is just making a bowl for his wife for their anniversary and he doesn't have enough experience to finish with the tool, then fine, there's nothing wrong with sanding."

Judy confesses to an occasionally ambivalent view about the fundamental nature of her work. "I guess it depends on what mood I'm in. If I just did a lousy show and I'm tired and I have to make 150 tops, I think I'm just a factory, a grunt worker. But if I'm doing a piece where everything works and it's really balanced, right then I feel that I'm an artist."

As an artist, she has given a great deal of thought to the placement of turning in the hierarchy of art. "I've always been

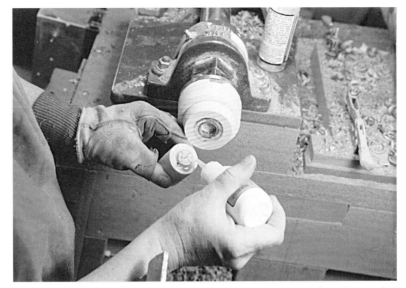

Judy applies cyanoacrylate glue to the spigot of the first piece of turning stock, which is then mounted into the hole cut into the waste block.

With a small fingernail gouge, Judy cuts a concave surface into the end of the turning stock. This surface will become the visible side of the first disc.

puzzled by the concept that only paintings express ideas. I have seen plenty of paintings that don't express ideas. Certainly, some of them do. But I disagree with the idea that only painting and fine art sculpture convey ideas.

"I guess I've never really understood the difference between art and craft. I understand the differences at the far ends of the spectrum. I can see that some things which are very functional, not very elaborate, might be craft items: maybe a top that's one of a hundred very

> "I don't want to spend a lot of time chainsawing big logs because it's just too demanding physically, so I've concentrated on smaller things."

similar pieces or a mug that a potter makes by the score. These won't have the kind of intellectual content of a really good painting, but I think there are a lot of places in between these where there can be disagreement.

"As Picasso said, 'If it's good, it's art; if it's not, who cares.' "

"I don't want to spend a lot of time chainsawing big logs because it's just too demanding physically, so I've concentrated on smaller things."

All art is autobiographical. Occasionally, that autobiographical content is easily seen, as, for example, in Rembrandt's many self-portraits. More often, however, the artist uses metaphor to tell his or her story. When Robert Frost speaks about a tuft of flowers or a stand of young birches, he is not simply talking about nature; he is telling us the story of his life.

However, for artists working with less representational imagery, the connections between the artist's life and the art-

ist's work can be more difficult to spot. Instead of presenting a straightforward recitation of his or her life, the artist may choose to create work in which the auto-biographical meaning is communicated obliquely, through the use of imagery that resonates rather than illustrates. The pristine cleanliness of Shaker design, for example, reveals no details of the Shaker's story of persecution, flight and communal living. It does, however, speak powerfully about the order and simplicity to which the Shaker communities aspired.

In a similar manner, Judy Ditmer's work tells the story of her life. She explains that this revelation of her autobiography starts with the notion of personal history, a characteristic she shares with the pieces she creates on her lathe.

"First there is the material," she explains. "Then there is what happened to that material. Maybe it was struck by lightning. Maybe it had a scar that healed over that created this grain here. Maybe it was cut a certain way.

"Then there is another factor: decision making. How do I attach this to the lathe? How much do I turn? How much of it should be left the way it came to me?"

Like the pieces she turns, Judy believes that "we all have our own inherent limitations and possibilities. On top of that, we have our own particular histories that further influence and limit those possibilities, and we also have the decisions we make which can affect what we do. To me, these pieces have a really powerful content."

Although this notion of personal history is one that we all share with the pieces she turns on her lathe, Judy sees much deeper connections between specific events in her own life and the lives of certain of her lathe creations.

Over the last decade, Judy has struggled with several serious and chronic health problems which have sapped her

With a specially ground parting tool, Judy cuts the first disc from the turning stock.

strength, interfering with her ability to work and diluting the pleasure she experiences in life. This, too, she has recorded in her lathe work, delineating the story with gouges and skews in the forms and surfaces she creates.

"I was doing really well until August. Then I had this intense retail show, with long hours outdoors in the heat. Now maybe that didn't have anything to do with it—my illness may have been coming on anyway—but I came home from that show sick, and I've been sick ever since. And right now I'm a little discouraged because I was doing so well earlier."

Complicating Judy's medical situation is her inability to find health insurance. "I suffer from clinical depression, and I'm on medication for that and probably will be for the rest of my life. I'm fine as long as I'm on the medication, but I can't get insurance because of it. I've had two companies tell me, 'Don't even bother to fill out an application. We won't insure you.' And I say, 'Why can't you insure me and just exclude the depression?' I could live with that because all I need is the medication, although that is expensive. But nowadays, they're just looking for an excuse to turn you down."

Her failure to find health insurance has not only required her to pay her health care costs out of her own pocket, it has also made finding a doctor difficult. She has learned through personal experience that some doctors are reluctant to see uninsured patients, a circumstance that further ensnarls her life. She says that there have been times, during her illnesses, when she would have chosen to change doctors if that option had been available.

Some people might have been overwhelmed by the difficulties Judy has faced, but because she is an artist, she has found ways to cope, turning often to her work not only for explication but also for inspiration.

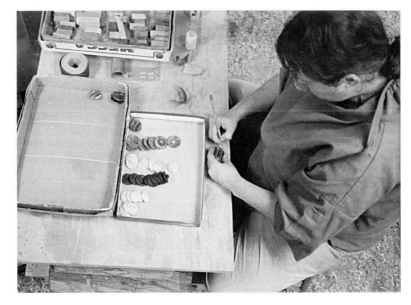

After the discs have been cut, she marks them prior to cutting them on the band saw. At this point, she begins to make decisions about how she will use the material in a particular production run, cutting around defects, choosing which discs will be left whole and which will be cut into halves and into quarters.

To illustrate this process, Judy tells a story: "Once I got this piece of beech, and I thought I was going to make a salad bowl out of it, all round and smooth. But when I put it on the lathe, I saw it was spalted, really far gone, very corky. But there was something about it I kind of liked, so I kept working on it. It was very difficult to turn because it kept wanting to fly apart. I kept turning it and turning it. Then I got tired, and I went to bed. Then the next day, I came into the shop, and I saw this piece and thought, 'Whoa, this is really good.'

"I feel like that piece taught me something really important: the difference

She very carefully feeds the discs past the blade on her band saw.

At this point, Judy sands the band-sawn edges of each piece using a line of lathe-mounted abrasive drums of varying diameters. Here, too, she is making decisions about how the final pieces will look, as a good deal of shaping can be done on these drums.

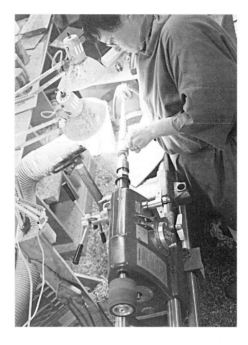

between acceptance and giving up, which was a very important issue for me at that point in my life, because I was very ill, and I was dealing with the fact that it didn't appear that I was going to be able to get well.

"Giving up is the end of everything. Acceptance is something different. Acceptance is where you say, 'No, this isn't what I thought it was going to be, and this isn't what I wanted it to be, but here is what it is.' And that's the same way that piece was: It wasn't what I thought it was going to be or what I wanted it to

be. But I went ahead and worked with it, and it turned out to be incredible. In fact, a lot of the work I did after that was informed by that bowl.

"When I look at the salad bowls, I see that idea manifesting itself in different ways because salad bowls have to have certain characteristics: Since people will put food in them, the wood has to be intact. I see salad bowls having this balance, this grace, this serenity, which is sometimes really difficult to achieve in life."

This doesn't mean that she necessarily feels peace and serenity during the turning of those bowls. "Sometimes making the bowl is very, very difficult, but when I look at a finished bowl, I don't see that. Here, too, is a connection with life: Sometimes I experience moments that are really difficult to deal with, but good things can come out of those times."

The Power of Acceptance

Popeye said it best: "I yam what I yam."

Maybe, if he could have taken the clay into his own hands, Popeye would have made himself taller or smarter. Or maybe he would've carved out a pair of normal forearms from the tattooed hams suspended from each elbow.

But Popeye realized that such things were beyond his power. He realized, too, that the only route to his own happiness was through the acceptance of himself just as he was: toothless, one-eyed, bowlegged. Like Popeye, we must find ways to accept ourselves as we are.

And this is the lesson that Judy Ditmer learned at her lathe. Sometimes the material is flawed. Sometimes it's scorched or split or spalted. But if we're patient, if we accept the material as it's given to us, there is the possibility of revealing the beauty that may be locked inside.

At the small disc sander on the left, Judy sands away the marks left by the abrasive drums.

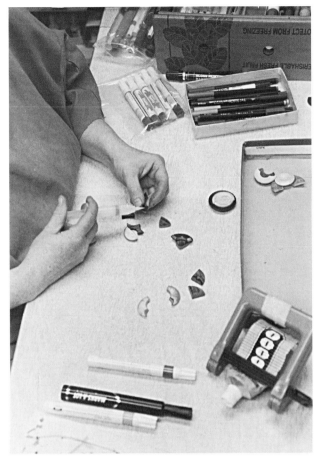

Using E6000 glue in a plastic syringe, Judy tacks together the pieces that will eventually become a set of earrings.

After the posts have been glued into place on the back of each earring, the posts are pressed into rubber earring backs press fit into the eyes of a series of cotter pins mounted in a stick of wood. The earrings are then sprayed with lacquer.

Judy sits in her shop behind the cardboard trays in which she keeps the pieces representing the various stages in her production process.

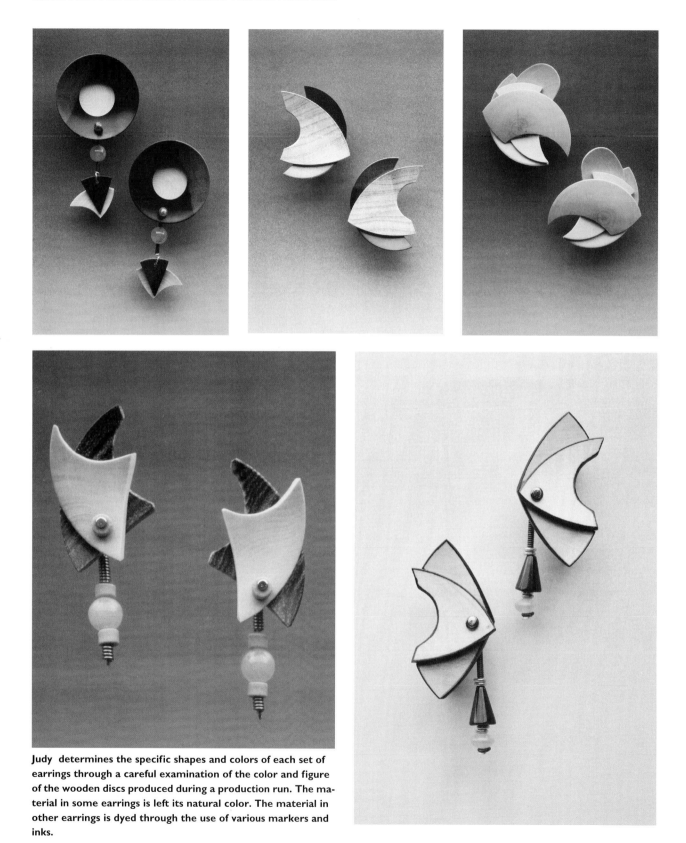

Judy determines the specific shapes and colors of each set of earrings through a careful examination of the color and figure of the wooden discs produced during a production run. The material in some earrings is left its natural color. The material in other earrings is dyed through the use of various markers and inks.

CHAPTER TEN

KERRY PIERCE

Production Runs in Your Shop

A herd of dining chairs grazes in the lawn beside my shop.

F O C U S : The craftspeople who have generously shared their stories in this book make a number of excellent suggestions for woodworkers considering the use of production-run methods in their own operations. To their suggestions, I would like to add six of my own.

When I was young, I worked in a mill that made bow windows and circular stairways for expensive homes. The mill employed 10 or 15 people, each of whom was given responsibility for a very specific set of tasks in the mill's production work.

At the bottom of the mill's status ladder was the laborer—usually someone very young and strong—whose task it was to take on all the really unpleasant jobs: to unload boxcars stuffed to the ceiling with hardwood, to fetch materials from the warehouse, to sweep.

Another man, one step up the status ladder, stood all day long, five and a half days a week, at an enormous table saw taking lumber from carts and placing it on the saw table where it could be engaged by the power feeder, in this manner ripping out stair treads and window mullions, sash stock and stair risers.

Another man framed in circular stairways. Another ran the sticker that created the miles of trim required by the mill's production.

Then at the very top of the status ladder were those craftsmen who did the fussy work of fitting together the fin-ished parts. These men were older and had already served their time, either in this mill or one like it. The younger men looked up to them and were also, in some cases, jealous of them. After all, these older craftsmen earned more money and enjoyed a status nearly equal to that of the mill's superintendent.

But even for those craftsmen at the top of the status ladder, the work could be monotonous, with any one day very much like any other. Although their jobs regularly provided them with the gratifying experience of demonstrating their hard-won manual skills, there was still—at least for my taste—too much of the assembly line flavor about their work.

Working at this mill was my first experience in production-run woodworking. I quickly realized that—at least as practiced in that mill—production-run woodworking wasn't something I wanted to do for the rest of my life.

Years later, in my own shop, I took another stab at production-run work. Having an order for one Hepplewhite-style huntboard (patterned after one drawn by Carlyle Lynch for *Fine Woodworking*), I decided to make five—two in cherry, one in oak, one in walnut and one in hickory, thinking that I could make better use of

Suggestion #1: Avoid shop situations in which the same individual is performing the same task day after day after day.

Suggestion #2: Schedule your workday so the most physically (and emotionally) taxing operations are performed in small chunks, preferably early in the day when bodies and psyches are at their freshest.

Three completed Enfield chairs stand in my storeroom awaiting a finish. Several front ladders and several back posts lean against one of the completed chairs.

This detail shows the heavily figured maple used in the construction of these chairs.

Suggestion #3: Be wary about making copies of large items on speculation. They are material- and labor-intensive, and can be difficult to sell.

machine setups and having what now seems like an unbelievable confidence in my ability to find customers for those extra huntboards.

Because the glued-up panels from which I would cut the tops, backs and sides would be too wide for my planer, I decided to work them down by hand, first with a roughing plane to level them, then with a jack plane to smooth out the hollows left by my roughing plane.

Happily, excited by the prospect of the money I would make from the sale of these huntboards, I selected lumber and ran it through my planer to reveal color and figure. I then glued the material up into the panels from which I would cut the necessary parts: five tops, five backs and ten ends.

Everything went smoothly until I started planing.

For almost a week, I stood at my bench and planed and planed and planed. I sharpened my irons and planed.

I waded through knee-deep drifts of shavings and planed.

My arms and shoulders ached. My fingers went numb. My hands were contorted into claws suitable only for the handles of my plane.

But finally, nearly crippled by several days of continuous hand planing, I did finish the huntboards.

I then delivered the one that had been ordered, and I did manage to sell another to a shop specializing in reproductions. But I was stuck with the other three. One now stands in our living room. Another went to a relative as a wedding present. The fifth is in my shop, where I use it as an extra workbench.

Four years ago, I took an order for eight dining chairs patterned after some made in the nineteenth century by members of a Shaker community in Enfield, Connecticut. The chairs were to be made of a combination of curly and bird's eye maple. In all, these chairs required the creation of over 160 parts, most of which were turned on the lathe.

That's a lot of hours at the lathe. Although I like to turn, I knew that my brain would begin to get foggy if I attempted to produce all those parts in one continuous orgy of lathe works. So I did a little planning and set up a shop schedule that permitted me to intersperse time at the lathe with time at the band saw and time at the workbench, breaking up my workday so I never put in more than an hour or two of continuous turning.

By that time, I had made enough chairs to know that sometimes a chair just doesn't work. The finials atop the back posts might be a bit misshapen or the stress of assembly might create a hairline crack in a post. Because of this, I made enough parts for nine chairs, rather than just the eight my customer had ordered, thinking that, if one chair didn't exhibit a satisfactory level of quality, I could include the extra copy among the eight my customer had ordered.

And sure enough, during the assembly process, as I squeezed rung tenons into mortises cut in a pair of back posts, I got a little frisky with my pipe clamp and cracked a post. It was a heartrending moment because that particular set of back posts had the most spectacular figure in the set. But it was not a catastrophic moment because I'd had the foresight to make parts for one extra chair.

I learned something else on that job, something that experience had already taught me but that I had somehow managed to forget.

As much as possible, I try to match up the figure in my slat stock. If, on a particular chair I have two slats exhibiting a quarter-sawn grain with a strong horizontal flow, I try to find a third slat with a similar flow. In the case of this particular set of chairs whose slats were all sawn from bird's eye maple, I also tried to match it up with similar bird's eye patterns.

When I got down to the last two chairs and looked at my last six slats, I realized that I had one slat that didn't match anything. No matter how I mixed and matched, I couldn't find two other slats that made sense when grouped with that odd one.

There was only one solution: I had to make another slat. Although that was the best possible answer to my problem, in terms of time and effort, it was very costly. I had to select another board, cut it to length, resaw it, plane it to the correct thickness, cut the profile on the band saw, shape the upper edge with a plane and steam-bend the slat to the correct curvature.

And each of these processes had to be set up. Individually. For just one slat. Clearly, I should have made extra slats.

Recently, I did a production run of candle boxes, their design loosely based on a Shaker original. The six boxes I made featured hand-cut dovetails, as well as hand-planed raised-panel lids and bottoms.

Although made in a production run, I wanted each box to have a one-of-a-kind feel. To achieve this, I did three things.

First, I used a variety of woods: cherry, walnut, curly maple and white pine. Several boxes were made of pieces cut from the same species of wood. Others, however, were made of a mixture of woods. For example, one of the cherry boxes was given a curly maple top, as was a box made from black walnut.

Second, each box was assembled with a different dovetail pattern. Some boxes had corners with five tails; others had corners with eight. I varied the width of the tails at a single corner, making some narrow and others wide. Too, on several

Suggestion #4: Build some insurance into your production runs: If you need a dozen copies of an object, make 13. If you need 25, make 27.

Suggestion #5: When making a production run of any complicated assembly, run extra copies of critical parts.

117

Suggestion #6: Within the limits of the production-run approach, look for techniques that will allow you to differentiate among the items in an edition.

boxes, I used one dovetail pattern on one end of the box and a different pattern on the other end of the box.

Last, I used a different type of pull on the lid of each box. One was a natural opening in the lid, left by a loose knot. Another was a dished-out semicircle, very similar to the pull on the Shaker original. Two others were more flamboyant shapes carved into soft white pine. The remaining two were shaped from bits of contrasting wood and then fitted into joints cut into the edges of the lids.

Together these techniques permitted me to create six very different candle boxes, although each side, each end, each bottom and each lid were made to the very same measurements. (Oh, yes. I did make an extra candle box but that seventh copy had a pull shape that I found a little clumsy.)

The Experience Factor

A good production run, like a well-built house, needs a blueprint. Materials and measurements must be specified. The necessary tools must be at hand. Work must be planned to proceed in an orderly fashion.

But that blueprint can't be too restrictive. It must suggest rather than prescribe. In this connection, experience comes into play. In all things, the craftsperson must be flexible enough to learn from the sometimes harsh experiences of production-run woodworking. It's never too late to learn something new. There's always time to stop and rethink a shop procedure.

Only in this manner can craftspeople be assured that their work will be accomplished with reasonable efficiency and an acceptable level of quality.

Sources of Supply

CONSTANTINE'S
2050 Eastchester Rd.
Bronx, NY 10461
(800) 223-8087

Although Constantine's offers only a small selection of power tools, the company is an excellent source of veneers, exotic woods and specialized hardware.

GARRETT WADE
161 Avenue of the Americas
New York, NY 10013
(800) 221-2942

Although focused on classical hand-tool operations, Garrett Wade's catalog does offer the Inca line of power equipment. Also, the catalog is beautifully presented and worth reviewing by anyone with an interest in woodworking.

GRIZZLY IMPORTS, INC.
2406 Reach Rd.
Williamsport, PA 17701
(800) 523-4777

Grizzly's line of imported equipment ranges from relatively modest-priced consumer-grade tools up to beefier types capable of sustained, heavy-duty work.

HARTVILLE TOOL
940 West Maple St.
Hartville, OH 44632
(800) 345-2396

Most appealing for woodworkers using production-run processes is a wide variety of accessories for routers and router tables.

KLINGSPOR'S SANDING CATALOGUE
P.O. Box 3737
Hickory, NC 28603-3737
(800) 228-0000

The Sanding Catalogue presents a fine selection of high-quality abrasive products and accessories.

LEE VALLEY TOOLS, LTD.
P.O. Box 1780
Ogdensburg, NY 13669-0490
(800) 871-8158

In addition to a solid selection of hand tools, Lee Valley's catalog presents a variety of toggle clamps that can be used in the construction of jigs and fixtures.

McFEELY'S
1620 Wythe Rd.
P.O. Box 11169
Lynchburg, VA 24506-1169
(804) 846-2729

Based on a square drive screw system, McFeely's line has expanded into power tools, abrasives, toy parts, etc.

MEISEL HARDWARE SPECIALTIES
P.O. Box 70
Mound, MN 55364-0070
(800) 441-9870

Meisel's catalog presents a nice variety of wooden parts useful for woodworkers interested in making toys and household goods.

SEARS POWER AND HAND TOOLS
20 Presidential Dr.
Roselle, IL 60172
(800) 377-7414

I don't think I've ever been in a shop that didn't have at least one Craftsman tool somewhere on the premises.

TOOL CRIB OF THE NORTH
P.O. Box 14040
Grand Forks, ND 58208-4040
(800) 358-3096

This catalog is filled with high-quality, name-brand merchandise: Biesemeyer, DeWalt, Makita and others.

TREND-LINES
135 American Legion Way
Revere, MA 02151
(800) 767-9999

Trend-Lines offers name-brand power tools and supplies at discount prices.

WOOD CARVERS SUPPLY, INC.
P.O. Box 7500
Englewood, FL 34295-7500
(800) 284-6229

Their selection of power carving tools could have application in some production shops.

WOODCRAFT
210 Wood County Industrial Park
P.O. Box 1686
Parkersburg, WV 26102-1686
(800) 225-1153

Although their beautiful catalog is focused on hand-tool operations, it also presents a generous selection of parts—clockworks, beveled mirrors, etc.—which may be of interest to the woodworker using production-run techniques.

WOODHAVEN
5323 Kimberly Rd.
Davenport, IA 52806-7126
(800) 344-6657

Woodhaven's catalog presents an impressive array of router accessories which are likely to have considerable application in a production shop.

WOODPECKERS, INC.
P.O. Box 29510
Parma, OH 44129
(800) 752-0725

Woodpeckers's catalog offers several Incra jigs which make possible a dazzling array of woodworking joints.

WOODWORKER'S HARDWARE
P.O. Box 180
Sauk Rapids, MN 56379
(800) 383-0130

This catalog offers a massive selection of name-brand cabinet hardware.

WOODWORKER'S SUPPLY
1108 North Glenn Rd.
Casper, WY 82601
(800) 645-9292

This very comprehensive catalog offers a bit of everything for the power-tool-based shop.

Index